MW00784336

Louis Poulsen

Louis Poulsen
First House of Light

TF Chan

A Brief History

Above: Copenhagen's first power plant, Gothersgade elektriske
Centralstation, opened in 1892 on Gothersgade, a stone's throw from
Louis Poulsen's eventual headquarters at Nyhavn 11.

A Brief History

THE EARLY YEARS

On 12 February 1874, when Ludvig Raymond Poulsen (1846–1906) founded the company that would eventually become Louis Poulsen, he could not have imagined the internationally renowned lighting brand that it is today, nor the influence it has had on Danish culture. For the company he founded did not deal in lighting at all (Denmark had yet to be electrified, so nighttime illumination would have been provided by fireplaces, candles and kerosene lamps) but rather in wine. There is little surviving information on The Copenhagen Direct Wine Import Company, as it was called, although it is known that it billed itself as the successor to another wine importer, Kornerup & Blad, and that it wasn't particularly successful. Ludvig was never admitted to the wine merchants' guild and had to move his company from one unfashionable address to another.

Ludvig's fortunes would change in the early 1890s, when electrical power arrived. The first power plants opened in 1891 in Odense, Denmark's third-largest city, and in 1892 on Gothersgade, a street in central Copenhagen. Sensing a new opportunity, and tapping into his connections with foreign suppliers, he opened a shop on Istedgade, in the western part of the city, selling lighting and electrical supplies—among its offerings were carbon-arc lamps, an early form of electrical lighting that involved running a current across two touching carbon electrodes that were then slowly pulled apart. One intermediary who purchased Ludvig's carbon-arc lamps in 1896 installed these in a town square in Randers, western Denmark, for a fee of 100 Danish kroner (DKK). He would later recall that to reassure the apprehensive customer, he offered to refund 10 DKK every time the lamps flickered. They didn't flicker at all and he received the full fee without deductions.

As his lighting and electrical supplies business grew, Ludvig was able to move it to the more centrally located Tordenskjoldsgade in Copenhagen a few years later. He also diversified his business, among other things selling scissors, grease guns, pig iron, crucibles, hoses and water meters to a clientele that likely consisted of many plumbers. It was around this time, in 1896, that his nephew Louis Julius Poulsen (1871–1934), a trained pharmacist, joined the company. An entrepreneurial spirit ran in the family: aside from working with his uncle, Louis also set up his own company in 1906 to sell corks, which in practical terms meant he had a machine that punched cylindrical holes in cork boards. The cork business was a rapid success: by the following year, he was importing cork from twelve different suppliers in Portugal and selling his products across Scandinavia. (The business continued until 1918, when breweries replaced cork stoppers with metallic caps, thus sounding its death knell.)

Louis Poulsen & Co a/s

Grundlagt 1874

Belysnings-afdeling

Hovedkontor:

NYHAVN 11 København K

Telefon central 1414

Aarhus afdeling:

Parkalle 15 Aarhus

Telefon 2 66 22

LISTE B 50 1953

In 1908, two years after Ludvig died, Louis merged the two businesses and relocated it to Nyhavn, the famous stretch of waterfront in central Copenhagen lined with multicoloured townhouses. Nyhavn 11, which would serve as the company's headquarters until 2006, had once been a sugar refinery. This was established by Ludvig Ferdinand Rømer (1714–76), who was a member of the Danish West India Company and eventually governor of the Danish Gold Coast (in modern-day Ghana). The building had been expanded since Rømer's time, but a monument to its sugary past remained in the form of an emblem above the gate, showing a small man with a sugar mould and sugarloaf.

THE ESTABLISHMENT OF LOUIS POULSEN & CO

The turning point of the company came when the young and ambitious Sophus 'Buski' Kaastrup-Olsen (1884–1938) ran into Louis Poulsen on Nyhavn. Like Poulsen, Kaastrup-Olsen came from an enterprising family. His grandfather, Christian Ludvig Olsen (1807–65), had established a high-end bakery that recruited bakers all the way from Vienna, designed an oven that he patented in Europe and the United States, and was eventually named baker to the Royal Court of Denmark. The family baking business continued to grow under the leadership of Kaastrup-Olsen's father, Johan Ludvig Waldemar Olsen (1842–97), who opened multiple branches and illuminated them with carbon-arc lamps. But Kaastrup-Olsen had no intention of taking this over. As a youth, he had aspired to a literary career, which he abandoned at the advice of Georg Brandes (a famed literary critic and co-founder of the daily newspaper *Politiken*), and eventually went to the United States and Germany to acquire a trade education. While in the USA, it dawned on him that electricity would play a prominent role in the future. Accordingly, in 1911, he purchased a 50 per cent stake in Louis Poulsen's electrical business for 10,000 Danish kroner (equivalent to around £83,000/US$105,000 today) and became a partner, establishing the company that would thereafter be known as Louis Poulsen & Co and become one of Denmark's most storied design houses. The name would remain after 1917, when Poulsen grew tired of business life, sold his shares to Kaastrup-Olsen and retired to a farm in western Denmark.

The business boomed in the few years following the First World War, as electric cables were laid across the country and electricity companies were established, giving a major boost to agriculture and industry, but by 1922 the Danish economy was in free fall. The country's largest private bank, Landmandsbanken, failed, 40 per cent of businesses went under, and Louis Poulsen was posting heavy deficits. It was around this perilous time that Kaastrup-Olsen first worked with Poul Henningsen (1894–1967)—a decision that would kick off a decades-long collaboration, reverse his company's decline, cement its role as Denmark's first house of light, and in doing so, make a significant mark on design history.[1]

Opposite: An aerial view of Nyhavn 11, Louis Poulsen's headquarters from 1908 to 2006, as shown on the cover of the brand's 1953 catalogue.

Overleaf, left page: Entries in the 1942 logo competition, which was won by architect Johan Pedersen. Overleaf, right page, clockwise from top left: The company's first logo in 1874 when it was named Kjøbenhavns Direkte Vin Import Kompagni; Louis Poulsen logos introduced in the 1920s, 1942 (by Pedersen), 1990s, 2023 and 1980s.

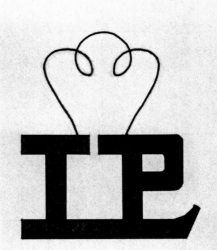

louis
poulsen

louis poulsen

POUL HENNINGSEN

Sophus Kaastrup-Olsen was a free thinker and cultural radical, who believed that the popularization of electricity provided opportunities for social empowerment. It is no surprise then that he would hit it off with Henningsen, following an introduction in 1924 via Poul's half-sister's husband, the architect Thorkild Henningsen (1884–1931).[2] Ten years younger than Kaastrup-Olsen, Poul Henningsen was the son of Agnes Henningsen (1868–1962), a writer and advocate for sexual freedom, and the novelist Carl Ewald (1856–1908), with whom she had an extramarital relationship. Henningsen's knack for innovation was evident from an early age—at sixteen, he made a self-pumping bicycle that won him a scholarship for young artists and inventors.[3] He studied to be an architect at Copenhagen Technical College but never graduated, choosing instead to focus his efforts on lighting design (although he would continue to dabble in architecture over the years—for example, building his own home out of prefabricated concrete blocks in Gentofte, north of Copenhagen, in 1937). Henningsen was also a prolific journalist and an outspoken champion of radical ideas, for whom design and social advocacy went hand in hand. He saw in Kaastrup-Olsen a kindred spirit: 'Here I met a man who was just as crazy as me, and a lot of good came out of it,' he described.[4]

Henningsen's first lighting designs, created between 1915 and 1920, may have followed traditional typologies, but nonetheless showed glimmers of innovation. When a family friend commissioned the then twenty-one-year-old Henningsen to renovate his Copenhagen home, the designer created a handcrafted pendant comprising a steel wire frame carrying pear-shaped prisms (upcycled from an old chandelier), and a red crystal sugar bowl in the centre—an early attempt at correcting the colour of light. Another operating principle that he explored at the time was repetitive shapes: using trumpet-shaped bowls across several lamps so they could form a cohesive lighting system.[5]

Above: Designer Poul Henningsen (left) as a youth, with his mother
Agnes Henningsen and his siblings.

Above: A 1921 pendant lamp by Henningsen, in the dining room of his sister-in-law Inger Kragelund in Aalborg. The design, which cast harsh shadows and bad light, was eventually replaced by a PH lamp.

A Brief History

More audacious was a pendant from 1921, which saw Henningsen experiment with metal shades for the first time. Initially developed for the dining room of his sister-in-law Inger Kragelund, a version of the lamp was also exhibited at the Artists' Autumn Exhibition (an annual open exhibition held at Copenhagen's Den Frie Centre of Contemporary Art) in 1921, within a pavilion that Henningsen designed jointly with the painter and ceramic artist Axel Salto (1889–1961). The globe-like form of the pendant was made up of shiny horizontal rings—brass in Kragelund's dining room and silver at Den Frie—which would simultaneously shield the light source from direct view and reflect light outwards. The outstanding problems with this pendant were that it distributed the same amount of light upwards and downwards, which is not particularly energy-efficient, and that it created a dark spot directly underneath.[6] Both points would be addressed in Henningsen's subsequent designs.

In parallel to the aforementioned experiments, Henningsen was also developing his principles of lighting, which remain a guiding force for the Louis Poulsen company today, followed closely by its in-house design team and its illustrious roster of contributing designers alike. He began to articulate these in a series of articles for *Politiken* from 1923 to 1924: 'It would appear that the intensity of light which technology has achieved relatively cheaply in recent years, has been achieved at the cost of the light's quality, beauty and purity,' he wrote in the final article, which he signed PH—the pen name that he eventually used for his principal designs, and by which he continues to be known in Denmark today. In Henningsen's view, the advent of the incandescent bulb, much more powerful than candlelight and kerosene lamps, called for lighting designers 'to improve the hygiene, economy and beauty of light by scientific means'.

By hygiene, Henningsen was not referring to cleanliness, but rather physical and psychological health. A naked incandescent bulb was too powerful to be viewed directly, as its glare would irritate the eye and cause fatigue while working. 'To be hygienic, modern light must generate considerably less glare than candlelight,' he wrote. Hygiene could be achieved through light fittings that shielded the bulb from direct view and distributed the light so that no area appeared too bright. This had to be considered hand-in-hand with economy, meaning that light should be directed where it was needed. In living rooms, for instance, he advocated for strengthening the light that shines downwards and, accordingly, weakening the light that shines upwards. As for beauty, he believed that the white light from incandescent bulbs was in many cases impossible to use. By filtering and reflecting light through various materials, the lighting designer could create a warmer light, ideal for 'homes, restaurants and other places where there is a demand for conviviality and festivity'. He further noted that good light should allow us to accurately perceive colour and textures, as well as form shadows, which are clear but not too sharp.[7]

1925 PARIS EXHIBITION

Henningsen's combination of practical experience and theoretical knowledge made him the ideal collaborator for Louis Poulsen, where the lighting catalogue had previously consisted of decorative fixtures and designs that simply placed the light source behind a shade. In spring 1924, the designer arrived at Nyhavn 11 for his first meeting with Kaastrup-Olsen, bringing along lamp drawings that featured layered shades. Unlike the shades in his globe-shaped lamp, these were curved to better distribute light. Although initially sceptical, Kaastrup-Olsen would commit to working with Henningsen that summer, knowing that Denmark would be participating in the International Exhibition of Modern Decorative and Industrial Arts in Paris the next year, and a series of national competitions would be held to select its representatives. Kaastrup-Olsen chose well—on 27 October 1924, Henningsen would win the competition's lighting prize (alongside his then collaborator Knud Sørensen, 1902–80), thus guaranteeing Louis Poulsen's participation in the 1925 exhibition. Months later, he would also be commissioned to oversee the lighting of the Danish sections of the exhibition, which presented Louis Poulsen with another high-profile opportunity.[8]

Henningsen moved to Brussels for a few months in order to find some peace and quiet to focus on the Paris Exhibition. There, he decided that his lamps for the exhibition would need frosted bulbs, so that light would emanate not just from the incandescent bulb's filament but rather be diffused across the surface of the bulb. He found a French factory to produce special bulbs of a specific size, with frosted surfaces and an operating voltage that would emit a warm light. He also created a series of ray direction drawings. These were sketches showing the cross-section of his lighting designs, with lines indicating how rays would emanate from the bulb's surface and be reflected in his curved shades. It took a month of trial and error—varying the curves of his shades and drawing out the rays accordingly—for him and Sørensen to arrive at the Paris lamp, which would be shown at the Louis Poulsen stand in Paris as well as illuminating the Danish exhibition halls. With its six silver shades, the Paris lamp directed a strong, even light downwards, which reduced in strength up the wall of its space. They additionally designed a globe-shaped lamp, 1 m (3⅓ feet) in diameter and with twelve curved shades, to be installed in the Danish National Pavilion, a red- and white-brick structure by the functionalist architect Kay Fisker (1893–1965).

Above: Henningsen's globe-shaped pendant on view at the 1925
Paris Exhibition in the Danish National Pavilion, by functionalist
architect Kay Fisker and featuring murals by painter Mogens
Lorentzen (1892-1953).

Top-left box:

ECLAIRAGE D'EXTERIEUR et D'INTERIEUR. SYSTEME P.H.
[Brevet en instance d'enregistrement]

Poul Henningsen   Louis Poulsen & C°.
Architecte   Articles Electriques.

COPENHAGUE, NYHAVN 11

ADRESSE TELEGRAPHIQUE: Elpeco, A.B.C Code (5 Edition) Boîte Postale 133&134

Poul Henningsen & Co   Louis Poulsen & Co
Arkitekt   Elektriske Artikler
KØBENHAVN NYHAVN 11
Patent anmeldt

INDVENDIG OG UDVENDIG BELYSNING SYSTEM P.H

Telegramadr. ELPECO A B C CODE (5 Edition)
Postbox 133 og 134

Top-right box:

ECLAIRAGE OBTENU AVEC DES HAUTES SUSPENSIONS - L U S T R E S -, MODELES 1,2,3

PRINCIPE ECONOMIQUE: Grande utilisation et bonne distribution de la lumière.

PRINCIPE HYGIENIQUE: Diminution de l'intensité si désagréable pour les yeux de la lampe à incandescence.

PRINCIPE ESTHETIQUE: Forme entièrement choisie d'après les qualités propres à l'éclairage électrique.

Lustre Modèle 3	Lustre Modèle 2	Lustre Modèle 1
Voir Tableau 2,3 et 4	Voir l'éclairage des sections danoises au GRAND PALAIS et ici	Voir Colonne 1 et 2
Une lampe 110 Volt Demi-watt 2000 bougies		Une lampe 110 Volt Mono-watt 50 bougies
Prix env. 1500 Frcs	Une lampe 110 Volt Demi-watt 1000 bougies Mono-watt 400 -"-	Prix env. 500 frcs
	Prix env. 1000 frcs	

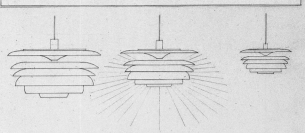

Middle-left box:

Tableau 1.   Eclairage à l'intérieur

ECLAIRAGE A L'INTERIEUR.   PRIX ET RENSEIGNEMENTS

L'éclairage des sections danoises au GRAND PALAIS - rez-de-chaussée et balcon - et celui du PAVILLON NATIONAL du DANEMARK, Cours la Reine, est aménagé par Monsieur Poul HENNINGSEN, Architecte, et par la Maison LOUIS POULSEN & C°. Tous les appareils d'éclairage de même que ceux exposés dans cette salle, sont à vendre, mais ne seront disponibles qu'après la fermeture de l'Exposition. D'autres appareils peuvent être fabriqué et livré dans un délai d'un mois. Les prix suivants sont calculés pour des pièces séparées. Au sujet de fourniture pour grandes salles ou d'éclairage extérieur, des propositions seront données à toute demande adressée à M.M. LOUIS POULSEN & C° Nyhavn 11, COPENHAGUE.

Tavle 1   Indvendig Belysning

INDVENDIG BELYSNING   PRISER OG OPLYSNINGER

Belysningen af de danske Afdelinger i Grand Palais, Stue og første Sal, samt af Danmarks Pavillon i Cour la Reine, er ordnet af Arkitekt Poul Henningsen og Firmaet Louis Poulsen & Co. Alle de til Belysningen anvendte Genstande er, ligesom de i dette Rum udstillede, til Salg, men er først til Disposition naar Udstillingen lukker. Indenfor en Maaned kan andre Eksemplarer fremstilles og leveres. De efterfølgende Priser er beregnet paa Salg af enkelte Eksemplarer. Ved Bestilling af flere Belysningsgenstande til store Rum, ved Spørgsmaal om udvendig Belysning eller Forhandling, fremsættes Tilbud ved skriftlig Henvendelse til Louis Poulsen & Co Nyhavn 11 Kbh.

Middle-right box:

Lysekrone Model 3	Lysekrone Model 2	Lysekrone Model 1
Se Tavle 2,3 og 4	Se Belysningen i de danske Afdelinger i Grand Palais og her	Se Søjle 1 og 2
En Lampe, 110 Volt Demiwatt 2000 Lys		En Lampe, 110 Volt Monowatt 50 Lys
Pris ca 1500 Frc.	En Lampe, 110 Volt Demiwatt 1000 Lys Monowatt 400 Lys	Pris ca 500 Frc.
	Pris ca 1000 Frc.	

HØJTHÆNGENDE BELYSNING: KRONEMODEL 1 2 3

Ø k o n o m i s k P r i n c i p : Stærk Udnyttelse og rigtig Fordeling af Lyset
H y g i e j n i s k : En Nedsættelse af Glødelampens for Øjet ubehagelige Glans
Æ s t e t i s k : Formen helt bestemt af de elektriske Lys særlige Egenskaber

---

Bottom-left box:

L A M P E S P O R T A T I V E S & L A M P E S S U S P E N D U E S: MODELES 1,2,3

PRINCIPE ECONOMIQUE: Grande utilisation et bonne distribution de la lumière

PRINCIPE HYGIENIQUE: L'éclairage peut être réglé. La lumière n'atteint pas directement l'oeil.

PRINCIPE ESTHETIQUE: Forme entièrement choisie d'après les qualités propres à l'éclairage électrique.

Lampe portative Modèle 1	Lampe portative Modèle 3	Lampe portative Modèle 2
Lampe suspendue Modèle 1	Lampe suspendue Modèle 3	Lampe suspendue Modèle 2
Voir Colonnes 3 et 6	Voir Colonnes 5 et 8	Voir Colonnes 4 et 7
Une lampe 110 Volts 50 bougies Monowatt	Une lampe 110 Volts 50 bougies Monowatt	Une lampe 110 Volts 50 bougies Monowatt
La lumière peut être réglée Faible éclairage vers le haut	La lumière peut être réglée Eclairage uniforme	La lumière peut être réglée Section d'éclairage variable
Lampe portative 500 frs Lampe suspendue 350 frs	Lampe portative 400 frs Lampe suspendue 250 frs	Lampe portative 300 frs Lampe suspendue 150 frs

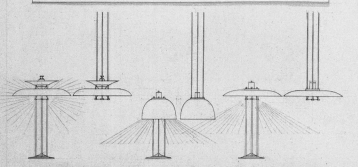

Bordlampe Model 1	Bordlampe Model 3	Bordlampe Model 2
Hængelampe Model 1	Hængelampe Model 3	Hængelampe Model 3
Se Søjle 3 og 6	Se Søjle 5 og 8	Se Søjle 4 og 7
En Lampe 110 Volt 50 Lys Monowatt	En Lampe 110 Volt 50 Lys Monowatt	En Lampe 110 Volt 50 Lys Monowatt
Lyset kan dæmpes Svagt Overlys	Lyset kan dæmpes Jævnt fordelt Lys	Lyset kan dæmpes Variabelt Lysfelt
Bordlampe 500 Frc. Hængelampe 350 "	Bordlampe 400 Frc. Hængelampe 250 "	Bordlampe 300 Frc. Hængelampe 150 "

BORDLAMPER OG HÆNGELAMPER.   M o d e l 1 2 3

Ø k o n o m i s k P r i n c i p : Stærk Udnyttelse og rigtig Fordeling af Lyset
H y g i e j n i s k : Lyset kan reguleres, Øjnene udenfor det stærke direkte Lys
Æ s t e t i s k : Formen helt bestemt af det elektriske Lys særlige Egenskaber

---

Bottom-right box:

ECLAIRAGE pour L'EXPOSITION. LUSTRES: MODELES 4 et 5

LUSTRE EN FORME DE BOULE   LUSTRE EN FORME DE CONE

L'éclairage du Pavillon du Danemark   La salle du fond au Grand Palais

Une lampe 110 Volts, Demiwatt 3000 bougies. Le lustre donne un éclairage vers le bas.

Une lampe 110 Volts, Demiwatt 1000 bougies, Eclairage sur les côtés.

Prix: 5000 frcs.   Prix: 200 frcs

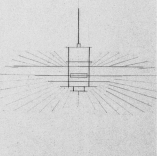

K U G L E F O R M E T K R O N E	K E G L E F O R M E T K R O N E
Belysningen af Danmarks Pavillon	Bageste Sal i Grand Palais
En Lampe, 110 Volt. Demiwatt 3000 Lys. Lysekronen er nedad lysende	En Lampe, 110 Volt. Demiwatt 1000 Lys. Lysekronen er udad lysende
Pris 5000 Frc.	Pris 200 Frc.

UDSTILLINGSBELYSNING KRONE MODEL 4 og 5

12989

Opposite: Explanatory text and diagrams from Louis Poulsen's stand at the 1925 Paris Exhibition, featuring (clockwise from top right) the Paris lamp; the globe-shaped lamp for the Danish National Pavilion; and smaller table and pendant lamps.

Above: Henningsen's Paris lamp, with six shades in German silver, was produced at the Lauritz Henriksen metal workshop.

When the Paris Exhibition opened in April 1925, Henningsen's lamps stood out for their form-follows-function approach. This was driven home by the format of the Louis Poulsen stand, which included not only lighting fixtures (the Paris lamp, alongside other recent designs by Henningsen and Sørensen), but also explanatory texts on the principles of hygiene, economy and aesthetics, and simplified versions of the ray direction drawings. As reported in a French magazine *La Renaissance de l'Art Français et des Industries de Luxe*, 'one notices that this lighting does not carry any form of adornment and stands out as a purely practical, cold and mechanical implement [...] It is more influenced by its content than a decorative exterior.'

Henningsen received one of thirty-six gold medals at the exhibition, and Louis Poulsen received a silver medal.[9] What would eventually become a four-decade collaboration was off to an auspicious start.

Above and opposite: A display of Danish porcelain at the Grand Palais, part of the 1925 Paris Exhibition, illuminated by Henningsen's Paris lamp.

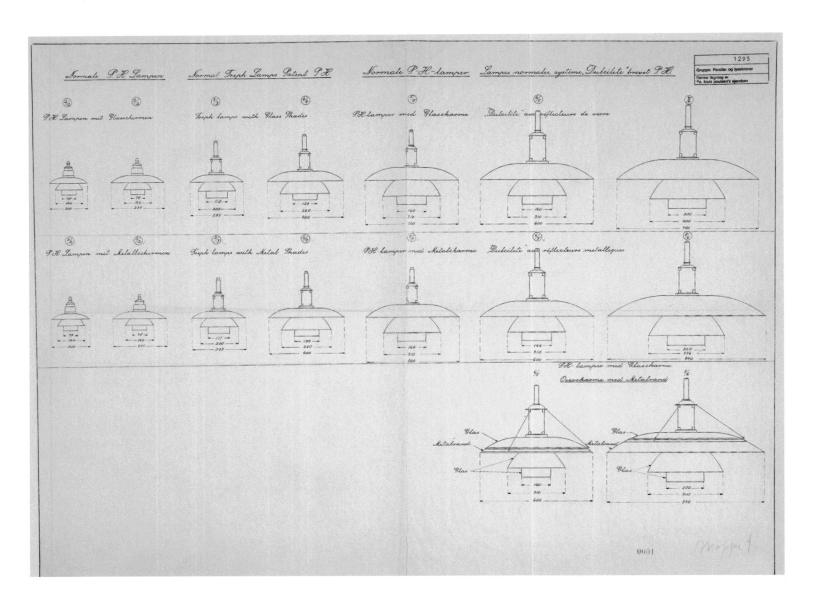

Above: A diagram showing PH pendant shade options in glass
and copper, c. 1929.

A Brief History

THE PH LAMP

The Paris lamp may have garnered international attention, but it was not glare-free: the choice of shiny silver for the lampshades meant that the lamp was dazzling when seen from below. After the exhibition, Henningsen set his sights on improving its design, deciding for instance that matte shades would help reduce glare. Accordingly, when he was asked to oversee the lighting for the new location of Copenhagen restaurant Schucani & à Porta a few months later, he adapted the Paris lamp to include slightly frosted gold plating on the shades.[10] More importantly, he examined the mathematical principles that made the Paris lamp an effective design and came to realize the merits of the logarithmic spiral. By drawing a logarithmic curve from the centre of the bulb, one could create an ideal shade that all light rays would hit at the same angle, thus facilitating the distribution of light.[11] Combining this with the use of multiple shades, to help focus light on the surfaces where it is needed, Henningsen arrived at a formula that would characterize his lighting designs in the decades to come.

In 1926, Henningsen reduced the number of shades in his lamp to three. This gave the lamp a more distinctive silhouette, and helped reduce manufacturing costs without compromising functionality. He decided that the top shade would be shaped like 'a flat plate', the middle shade like 'a slanted bowl' and the bottom bowl like 'a deep cup'[12]—altogether ensuring that a more concentrated light would be directed downwards and a more diffuse light outwards.

The new three-shade design, first implemented in pendant form at Copenhagen's Forum (see page 60), was soon developed into a complete PH lamp system, with different sizes, shade interiors (white, silver-plated and gold-plated) and finishes ranging from matte to shiny, to suit different purposes. An opal glass version was also introduced, with sandblasted undersides that ensured 12 per cent of the light would penetrate the shades and be diffused into the room, while the rest would be reflected in the same way light was reflected in a metal shade. The opal glass version would exceed its metallic counterparts in popularity, becoming the default image of the three-shade PH lamp. It was possible to combine materials within the same lamp: a metallic top shade with glass middle shade and bottom bowl, for instance, would spread light over a larger area than a set of pure metallic shade.[13]

Henningsen also devised a number system to indicate the various sizes in which PH shades were available: PH 4/4, PH 4/3, PH 2/1, and so on. The first digit indicated the diameter of the top shade (4, for instance, indicated a diameter of 400 mm/15¾ inches), while the second digit corresponded to the proportions of the middle shade and bottom bowl. Matching digits would mean that the three shades were in the ratio 3:2:1; a smaller second digit would mean the middle shade and bottom bowl were in the sizes one would expect for that digit (for example, a PH 4/3 fixture would have a 400 mm/15¾ inch diameter top shade, matched with the middle shade and bottom bowl from a PH 3/3). The option of smaller middle shade and bottom bowl would give the overall design a lighter feel, which was recommended for low-hanging use.[14] This sizing system was fully developed by 1926, and accompanied by light distribution curve diagrams that indicated the direction and intensity of light offered by each combination. The following year saw Louis Poulsen add PH table and wall lamps to its catalogue, with the same three-shade design.[15]

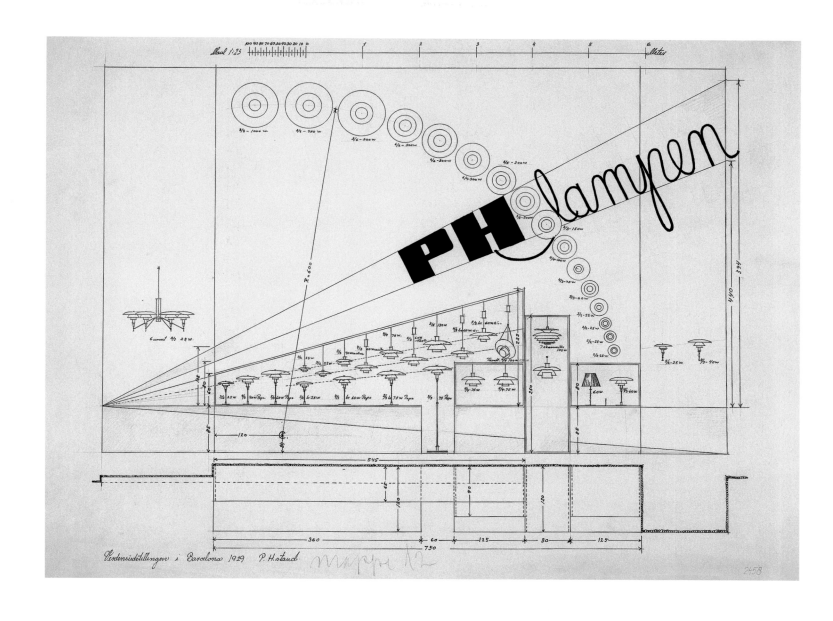

Above, a plan of the Louis Poulsen stand at the 1929 International Exposition in Barcelona, Spain, showing the whole range of PH lamps with all shade sizes and lamp types (table, pendant and floor). The stand also included a traditional pleated lamp to accentuate the modern nature of Henningsen's designs.

Opposite: Three PH table lamps from 1927: (from left) The 4/3 with green/bronze top shade and opal glass middle shade and bottom bowl; the 5/3 with opal glass shades; and the 3/2 with red/bronze shades.

33

The PH lamp was a rapid success and ensured that by 1927, five years after Denmark's economic collapse, Louis Poulsen was getting back on its feet.[16] It helped that the lamp found a loyal following among leading international architects such as Ludvig Mies van der Rohe (1886–1969) and Le Corbusier (1887–1965), who respectively used it at Villa Tugendhat in Brno, Czech Republic, and Villa Savoye outside Paris.[17] In 1926, when the lamp first appeared in Louis Poulsen's catalogue, the company didn't have much of an export business. By 1929, it had a network of 375 dealers, in locations as wide-ranging as Bergen in Norway, Cape Town, Lima and Manila.[18] So popular was the system that Louis Poulsen's local suppliers, such as the Lauritz Henriksen metal workshop, could no longer keep up with demand: glass components and leg frames for table lamps were outsourced to Germany, where they would continue to be produced until the onset of the Second World War.[19]

Opposite: The main living area at Mies van der Rohe's Villa Tugendhat in Brno, Czech Republic, featuring three-shade PH lamps with opal glass shades, and Mies van der Rohe's Barcelona, Tugendhat and MR Lounge chairs.

Above: A three-shade PH lamp with opal glass shades at Villa Tugendhat.

Above and opposite: Recent reissues of three-shade PH lamps with pale rose shades, (from left) the PH 2/2 Question Mark table lamp; reflection of the PH 3/2 table lamp; and the PH 2/1 table lamp.

A Brief History

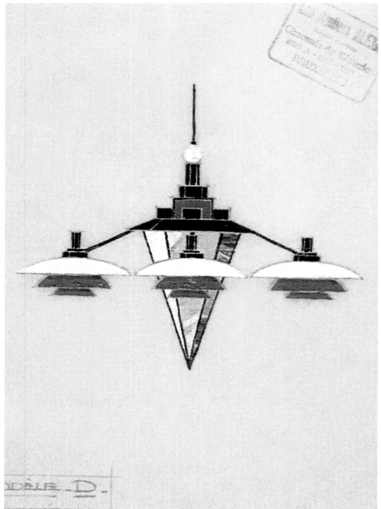

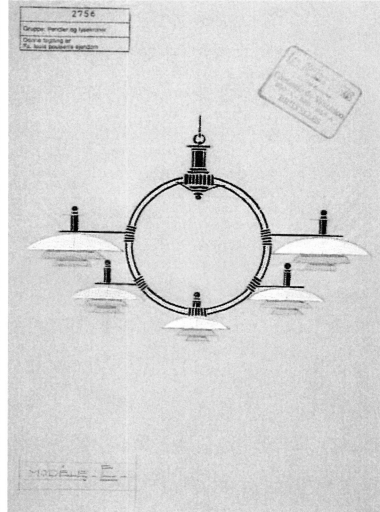

Above and opposite: A series of sketches, produced by Belgian company Les Ateliers Alexis, showing imaginative lighting designs involving the three-shade PH system and intended for Art Deco interiors.

The 1930s would see simplified construction and industrial manufacturing to bring prices down, and in parallel, a more extensive range of PH lamps to suit different tastes.[20] The white opal shades, in combination with the low lighting levels that most people had at home, resulted in a rather cool light, so red, amber and yellow glass shades were introduced to create a cosier ambience. Another development, which Henningsen regarded with ambivalence, was the introduction of decorative styles: small lamps for dressers and bedside tables with more traditional construction, and rather ornate chandeliers, some of them even with crystal prisms. A series of sketches produced by a Belgian company, Les Ateliers Alexis, included such bewildering designs as an inverted pyramid with three stacked PH fixtures and a crystal orb at the bottom, and a suspended conical helix with a large PH pendant fixture at its base and five successively smaller fixtures installed along the helix. These could well have been made, as Louis Poulsen was able to create custom-designed lamps for its customers. Such flexibility certainly contributed to the PH lamp's popularity, and offered a financial salve when the company's export revenues were falling amid a global recession.[21] At the same time, there is no denying that it complicated the lamp's original triumph of function over form.

Wartime rationing and shortages put an end to the wide range of options, but also brought forth new innovations. In 1943, to cope with shortages of glass, Louis Poulsen released PH lamps with three-layered shades in pleated paper, made by female Danish refugees in Sweden,[22] where Henningsen went into exile from that year until the end of the war. The PH lamp catalogue would once again expand in the mid-1950s and take on more new expressions, most notably with the introduction of the 1958 PH 5 pendant, which would surpass its predecessors to become the best-selling PH lamp ever.[23]

Opposite, above: A sketch of the 1943 PH Plissé lamp, made in pleated paper to cope with wartime glass shortages.

Opposite, below: Poul Henningsen, his wife Inger and friend Robert Soskin gathered around a dining table in Stockholm, under a PH Plissé lamp.

A Brief History

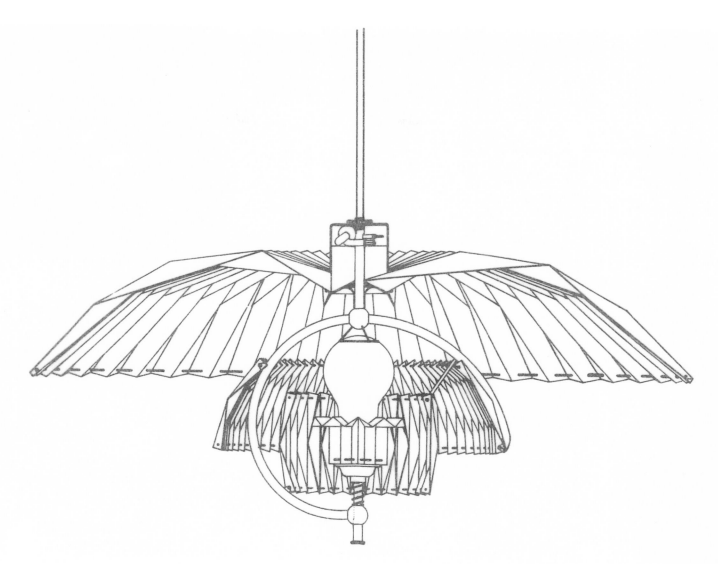

Above: Henningsen at the opening of the Louis Poulsen showroom at Nyhavn 11 on 25 October 1939.

Opposite: Illustrations of the Nyhavn showroom, featuring the three-shade PH lamp during the day and by night.

A Brief History

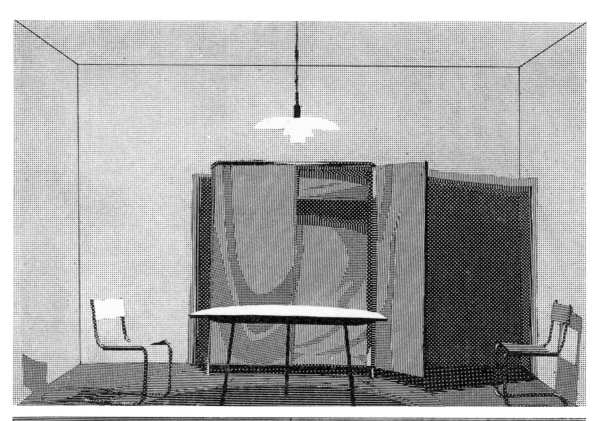

THE PH 5 LAMP

Despite its name, the PH 5 is in fact a four-shade pendant lamp, the '5' representing the 500 mm (20 inch) diameter of the top shade. In devising this design, Henningsen was addressing a flaw in the original PH lamps— that its glare-free properties depended on the light source being situated in a particular spot within the shade, which often necessitated professional installation considering that light bulb sizes were not yet standardized at the time. Not that standardization was an unadulterated good—whereas mushroom-shaped reflector bulbs were common in the 1920s, by the 1950s light sources were almost universally bulbous in form. This meant a mirror image of the filament would appear in the bulb neck, compounding the problem of glare. Writing in Louis Poulsen's magazine, *LP Nyt,* in April 1958, Henningsen expressed his frustration that bulb manufacturers were not concerned with producing light that was conducive to the wellbeing of the human eye: 'I have accepted fate, and with Louis Poulsen's permission I have designed a PH fixture, which can be used with any light source, Christmas lights, and 100 W metal filament bulbs.'[24]

The PH 5 saw the original three-shade system joined by a trumpet-shaped shade at the top, as well as two internal shades (only visible from a low angle), which allow rays to be reflected in the same way regardless of where the centre of the light source is. In other words, no matter what bulb the user chose, the light would remain entirely glare-free. With this design, Henningsen also wished to improve the colour reproduction characteristics of the light source. By colouring the internal shades in red and blue, corresponding to the parts of the colour spectrum where the eye is less sensitive, he subdued the light in the yellow-green region in the middle of the spectrum, where the eye is more sensitive. An additional bottom plate ensured that the light source would be concealed completely. All the shades were made in aluminium, for ease of manufacturing and to keep prices low, and held in place by brass spacers. (In 1994, the bottom plate was replaced by a piece of frosted glass, to let out more light at the bottom, considering that newly popular energy-saving bulbs mostly emitted light horizontally.) The resulting lamp, which gives a focused, but nonetheless soft and warm downward light, as well as a more diffuse sideways light, quickly became a staple of Danish homes, and for a while, one of the best-selling lamps in the world.[25]

Opposite: From Louis Poulsen's 2019 collection, variations of Henningsen's PH 5 lamp, designed six decades earlier.

Overleaf: Henningsen at home with a PH 5 lamp. The 1962 Contrast lamp appears in the background.

A Brief History

THE SPIRAL LAMP

While the PH and PH 5 lamps were characterized by their simplicity, Henningsen also created more elaborate lighting designs for Louis Poulsen, which nonetheless adhered to the principle of form-follows-function. This includes the world-renowned PH Artichoke lamp, designed in the same year as the PH 5 and discussed in Chapter 3, as well as the 1942 Spiral lamp, commissioned for the main hall at Aarhus University, which was 19 m (62 feet) high. In the case of the latter, the architect C. F. Møller (1898–1988) had outlined some balloon-like objects in his drawings and then approached Henningsen for the actual design. Henningsen suggested having spiral lamps, which looked as though they were drawn in one long stroke. The resulting design, which first appeared at the Artists' Autumn Exhibition in 1942 but wasn't produced until after the war, was a spiral shade, around 107 cm (42 inches) high and shaped like a water drop. The spiralling layers were uniformly spaced to give the illusion of simplicity. What made its construction particularly complex was Henningsen's insistence that the light—emanating from a bulb at the bottom of the lamp—should be reflected at different angles depending on the position of the shade, so as to illuminate the hall effectively. As he wrote in the November 1942 issue of *LP Nyt*, 'The shape is geometric and the light strikes all the parts of the spiral, which are illuminated at the same angle, reflecting it out into the room in the same way.'[26] In other words, the spiral begins at the top at an oblique angle, then flattens to a horizontal position near the centre, and eventually gathers at the bottom at an opposite angle, all to ensure that the resulting light is concentrated in the lower section of the hall.

Cutting the aluminium pieces and soldering them together into a coherent spiral, supported by three internal metallic arms, proved enormously difficult and time-consuming. This ultimately meant that the Spiral lamp could not be put into wider production. But the level of care that Henningsen devoted to an apparently simple design has resulted in its enthusiastic critical reception—an example is on display at Copenhagen's Designmuseum Danmark as part of the long-term exhibition *The Magic of Form: A Journey Through Danish Design History*,[27] and when another example came up for auction at Christie's in 2017, the lot essay called it 'one of the purest expressions of Henningsen's technical virtuosity, where its simplicity and purity of form reveal the perfectionist artistry of its conception'.[28]

Above: Henningsen's Spiral lamp, designed for the main hall at
Aarhus University by architect C. F. Møller.

LOUIS POULSEN TODAY

Both the PH and PH 5 lamps remain in production today and count among the most widely recognized designs in Louis Poulsen's catalogue, alongside the AJ lamp by Arne Jacobsen and the Panthella lamp by Verner Panton (see pages 126 and 169). The regular introduction of new colour variants (there are currently seventeen options for the PH 5[29]) and reissues of PH designs such as the curved-stemmed PH 2/2 Question Mark table lamp (designed in 1931 and reissued in 2021)[30] attest to their enduring relevance. Nonetheless, the story of Louis Poulsen is also the story of other design collaborations, which have ranged from the titans of mid-century Danish architecture and design, including Jacobsen and Panton, to contemporary talents such as Louise Campbell and Øivind Slaatto (see pages 202 and 217). Since Henningsen's time, these designers have worked for Louis Poulsen on a freelance basis, often contemporaneously, in close dialogue with the brand's in-house design team who help deliver their vision into reality. In some cases, lamps have been developed for specific buildings and, in response to popular interest, introduced into the company catalogue; in other cases, they have been initiated as standard products. Either way, as subsequent chapters will demonstrate, the designs have continued to follow Henningsen's ethos in their union of purpose and shape—or as the company slogan goes, 'we design to shape light'.[31]

The PH 5 played a crucial role in reviving Louis Poulsen's fortunes, which suffered during the Second World War, especially as Henningsen's vocal opposition to Nazism prompted the company to avoid working for the government during the five-year German occupation of Denmark.[32] The 1960s and 70s saw the company grow rapidly as it bought up smaller competitors across the country and opened its first overseas subsidiaries—in West Germany in 1962, France in 1964 and Sweden in 1975.[33] International expansion stepped up following the company's listing on the Copenhagen Stock Exchange in 1977, notably in the United States and Japan, which continue to rank among the brand's key markets. And in light of a long tradition of creative exchange between Denmark and Japan (Danish artists were among the first in the West to engage with Japanese art in the late nineteenth century, and shared the Japanese affinities for functionalism and simple beauty),[34] Louis Poulsen has brought Japanese design collaborators Shoichi Uchiyama and nendo on board in recent years (see pages 222 and 225). As Oki Sato, chief designer of nendo explains, 'there is a strong connection between Scandinavian design and Japanese design, especially about materials, natural materials such as wood, stone or fabric, and the respect for craftsmanship. I guess that is all linked by light. The quality of the light that Japanese people prefer, it's similar to the environment in Scandinavian countries as well. It's about natural light, how to bring the natural light into the interior. But it's not about direct light, it's softly diffused light'.[35]

Opposite, above: A 1957 PH 3/2 Water Pump Floor lamp with amber coloured glass. It was immediately dubbed 'the Water Pump' due to its adjustable arm.

Opposite, below: A 2019 limited-edition reissue of the Water Pump lamp.

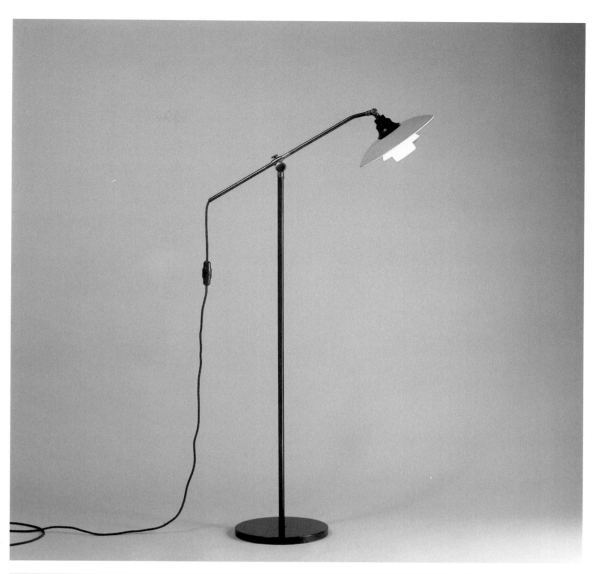

As with other key players in the industry, Louis Poulsen has placed an increasing emphasis on sustainability in the past decade. In this, the brand had a head start based on the enduring nature and high-quality manufacturing of its older designs, particularly the PH and PH 5 lamps. The company has laid out three key strategies to achieve its commitment to 'design for the planet'. These include designing a decarbonization strategy across its own operations and its value chain (from sourcing to disposal), implementing an eco-design framework to minimize a product's environmental impact from cradle to grave, and mapping and assessing the sustainability credentials of its suppliers. In parallel, Louis Poulsen is also stepping up its community engagement through strategic partnerships with vocational schools, universities and other non-governmental institutions, and affirming its commitment to diversity and inclusion. All of these bring the company in line with the United Nations Sustainable Development Goals (SDGs)—a shared blueprint for peace and prosperity with 2030 as its target year.[36]

An SDG sub-target that is particularly relevant for Louis Poulsen is the substantial reduction of waste generation through prevention, reduction, recycling and reuse. In 2020, the brand estimated that it was producing 1.75 kg (4 lb) waste per product. This number was brought down to 1.27 kg (3 lb) in 2021; at the time of writing, the aim is to further lower it to 1 kg (2¼ lb) by 2023. And while Louis Poulsen's in-house production has grown significantly in recent years—in 2022, it produced around 325,000 products at its factory in Vejen in south Denmark, compared to 213,000 in 2019—the brand managed to reduce its total energy consumption by 3 per cent during this time.[37]

Louis Poulsen's pilot take-back scheme, called Retake, is of particular interest from a consumer perspective. This launched in 2021 with the PH 5 Retake, whereby Louis Poulsen sourced and refurbished vintage or imperfect PH 5 lamps, stripping them of their painted finish to expose the raw aluminium and steel, and simply adding a dry lubricant. As a result of the stripping process, the aluminium surfaces vary in tone, whereas the lower steel shades will rust and patinate beautifully over time, offering further incentive for consumers to keep them for as long as possible. While the first batch was available only in Denmark, the brand is now working on expanding the Retake programme's international reach.[38] It also hopes to expand the Retake concept into its larger product portfolio and establish repair shops for consumers to bring in their old Louis Poulsen lamps to be retrofitted with contemporary hardware and sustainable light sources. As the brand's director of product and design Monique Faber explains, 'We want our lighting to become part of your history. So that when you pass on your lighting to the next generation, you are not only leaving them an object but also bequeathing them a legacy of good light, and of good design. A Louis Poulsen lamp should be treasured more and more the older it becomes.'[39]

Opposite: Launched in 2021 and stripped of their painted finish, the PH 5 Retake lamps feature exposed raw aluminium and steel, which patinate beautifully over time.

A Spirit of Democracy

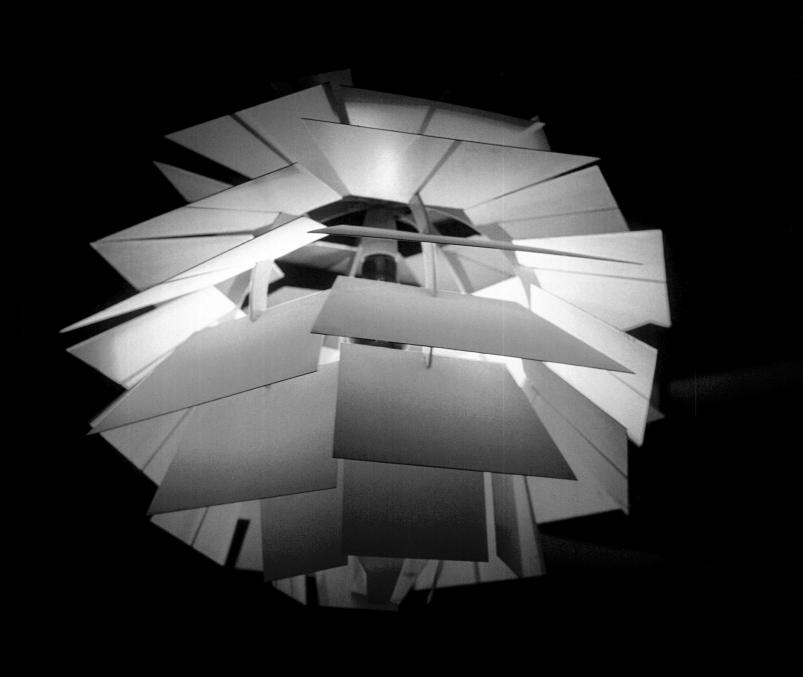

DESIGN FOR THE PUBLIC GOOD

First-edition Louis Poulsen lighting has fetched astronomical prices at auction in recent years: at the Important Nordic Design sale at Phillips London in November 2011, a 1955 Spiral wall light that Poul Henningsen had created for the Scala cinema and concert hall in Aarhus sold for a remarkable £253,250,[1] while his 1959 *House of the Day after Tomorrow* ceiling light, characterized by its white, yellow and red painted aluminium shades, went for £193,250.[2] It is a reflection of how well Henningsen's lighting for Louis Poulsen, alongside other icons of mid-century Danish design, has endured at home and achieved renown abroad. But, as the design historian Lars Dybdahl points out in *101 Danish Design Icons* (which has two entries dedicated to Henningsen, 'The economics of light' and 'Design critique on every scale'), 'rather than dazzling with an exceptional design-conscious attitude, the icons in this category have usually won on popular appeal, based on straightforward credibility in functionality'.[3] Henningsen saw design and architecture as social endeavours, and his lighting, alongside journalistic and other creative pursuits, often advanced a democratic agenda in a then somewhat conservative Denmark. These efforts have had a lasting influence on the Louis Poulsen brand, and may even have played a role in the building of his country's social democracy.

Prior to his collaboration with Louis Poulsen, Henningsen was already working on lighting projects for the public good. In 1919, the same year he founded his design firm, he created a street lamp for Copenhagen Energy—a glass cylinder topped with a large enamel shade, and with interior shades that directed light at oblique downward angles.[4] The design, which was a departure from the gas lamps that traditionally populated Copenhagen's streets, was unpopular. 'The papers wrote that it resembled a prune on a crochet hook,' Henningsen would later recall in a 1964 short film, *PH lys*. Nonetheless, it wound up being used on Slotsholmen (the island within Copenhagen where Christiansborg Palace, the seat of the Danish government, is located) for half a century, and Louis Poulsen took on production from the mid-1940s to 1967.[5]

Opposite: Poul Henningsen's *The House of the Day after Tomorrow* ceiling light, a limited edition of twenty created by Louis Poulsen for a 1959 exhibition imagining an ultramodern home.

A Spirit of Democracy

A Spirit of Democracy

Opposite: Henningsen's 1955 Spiral wall light for the Scala cinema and concert hall in Aarhus.

Above: Henningsen's street lamp for Copenhagen Energy, installed on Christiansborg Slotsplads, on the island of Slotsholmen in central Copenhagen. By the time of this photo, the interior shades had been removed as they swallowed more light than improved it. Copenhagen Energy removed the bottom four shades, leaving a main shape with a completely different lamp.

FORSLAG TIL BELYSNING I KØBESTÆVNETS BYGNING MED 42 ARMATURER.

2466

Gruppe: Diverse

Denne tegning er
Fa. louis poulsen's ejendom

2612

It is also noteworthy that long before Henningsen's lamps became a staple of Danish homes, they were installed in notable public spaces throughout Denmark. In autumn 1925, just six months after the Paris Exhibition, Henningsen was invited to create lighting for a new indoor arena in Frederiksberg (in the western part of Copenhagen) called the Forum, designed by Oscar Gundlach-Pedersen (1886–1960). This was a last-minute project. By Henningsen's recollection, he was given only eight days to come up with the design, and the prototype—created by metal manufacturer Lauritz Henriksen for Louis Poulsen—was delivered to Gundlach-Pedersen just five minutes before the deadline for tenders. The architect was impressed, writing that compared to the other two entrants, Henningsen's design 'provided a much stronger direct impression of festive lighting [...] and they also spread the light, which meant, e.g. vertical surfaces were particularly powerfully lit despite long distances from the lamps.' The Forum lamps remained in place during the Nazi occupation until August 1943, when the building was blown up by Danish resistance saboteurs so it could not be used to house German troops.[6]

Above: A drawing illustrating Henningsen's early plans for lighting the Forum arena in Frederiksberg, with forty-two glass lamps hung along the perimeter and two large fittings near the arena's centre.

Opposite: Henningsen's copper Forum lamps in the completed space, configured for a boxing match and a car show respectively in 1926 and 1927.

A Spirit of Democracy

Other public spaces followed suit: department stores, banks, museums (including the Danish Museum of Decorative Art, a predecessor of the Designmuseum Danmark, which moved into a former hospital building in 1926 following a renovation by the father of Danish Modern design, Kaare Klint, 1888–1954)[7] and train stations (Aarhus Station introduced three eighteen-armed chandeliers with PH shades in 1929,[8] which remain in place today;[9] alas, Copenhagen Central Station never adopted Henningsen's design due to a newspaper campaign that warned against 'modern horrors'). The designs also found rapid success outside Denmark: Finnish architect and designer Alvar Aalto (1898–1976), who would become a lifelong friend of Henningsen's,[10] used PH lamps in the auditorium of a 1928 building in Turku, south-west Finland;[11] the lamps were installed at the Bauhaus in Dessau, Germany;[12] while at the 1929 International Exposition in Barcelona, Spain, they received the highest commendation.

Three-shade PH lamps, installed (above) at the Southwestern Finland Agricultural Cooperative Building in Turku, Finland, built in 1927–8 by Alvar Aalto, and (opposite) at Copenhagen's Danish Museum of Decorative Art, following its 1926 renovation by Kaare Klint.

Lesser remembered, especially in an international context, is the fact that because of their effectiveness and relative affordability, PH lamps also found favour in less glamorous spaces, where lighting decisions would rarely be determined by aesthetics. Looking through the Louis Poulsen archives, we can see the lamps used in factory floors, hospitals, orphanages and even greenhouses (of the functional sort, as opposed to those in botanical gardens). Following the same principles as the PH lamp, Henningsen even developed a special Tennis lamp in 1927, around the time sports halls started appearing across Denmark, necessitating new forms of artificial lighting that would properly illuminate the pitch without expending too much light on the walls and ceiling. Henningsen's solution was to replace the usual frosted white undersides of the shades with a half-glass aluminium coating, to better reflect light; and to cut a hole in the top shade to insert a piece of frosted glass, in order to reduce glare. Finally, as the Tennis lamp was designed to be suspended diagonally, he cut off part of the lower shade, so there would be more light directly underneath the lamp.[13] The lamp was notably used in Copenhagen's K.B. Hallen, which was Europe's largest privately owned sports facility when it opened in 1938. There, it remained in place until the hall burned down in 2011.[14]

Opposite: The opal glass lamp 4/4 and opal table lamp 5/2, from the PH lamp system, at a Copenhagen branch of Landmandsbanken, then Denmark's largest private bank, in 1927.

Above: From the same year, further opal glass lamps from the PH system at the Copenhagen municipal children's home on Ingerslevsgade.

A Spirit of Democracy

Opposite: A close-up of the Tennis lamp, developed in collaboration with tennis player Einar Middelboe, with part of the lower shade cut off so there is more light directly underneath the lamp.

Above: Henningsen's Tennis lamps illuminating K.B. Hallen, pictured during the Copenhagen Open in spring 1994.

WRITING AND FILMMAKING

Henningsen's activities outside the design field corroborate this ongoing interest in public space. He began writing for Denmark's largest daily newspaper *Politiken* in 1921, and was soon appointed the paper's first architecture critic,[15] becoming a leading champion of societal concerns in a time of rapid urban development. He was particularly outspoken in his criticism of short-term thinking among municipal authorities who were in charge of urban planning. Five years later, Henningsen would channel his opinions into his own magazine, *Kritisk Revy* (*Critical Review*), which included Danish, Norwegian and Swedish architects and left-wing intellectuals on its editorial team, and was unabashed in its challenging of the cultural establishment.[16] As Dybdahl, the design historian, describes, '*Kritisk Revy* championed a new social awareness, advocating utility and democratic responsibilities in relation to urban planning, architecture and design, practising a functionally driven aesthetic design critique on every scale and calling for realistic approaches to replace conservatism and social democratic snobbery.'[17]

Opposite: A still from *PH lys*, a 1964 short film directed by Ole Roos (1937–2018) in which Henningsen explained the lighting principles that guided his designs.

Above: Henningsen at the Allé-Scenen theatre in Frederiksberg with his PH 5 lamps hanging above.

A Spirit of Democracy

This position was made clear from the inaugural issue, in which Henningsen penned a review of *Vers une architecture* (*Towards a New Architecture*; 1923) by Le Corbusier, which had recently been translated into German: he criticized the Swiss architect's design approach for neglecting the social tasks of architecture and city planning, and took the opportunity to elucidate his own vision of 'democratic art': 'With perfect justice we can assert that only democratic art is of value today, and only the kind of art that appeals to and is understood by the masses is modern in the proper sense of the word.'[18]

Kritisk Revy shuttered in 1929, the official explanation being that the most important points had been made on all key fronts.[19] (This claim did not quite align with its editorial focus, which expanded to include literature, music, theatre, film and more. Among its more eyebrow-raising features was a discussion on the pedagogical value of pornography.)[20] Henningsen would find other outlets for his cultural critique, such as a 1933 book *Hvad med Kulturen?* (*What About Culture?*), which advocated ambitious reforms to create a more progressive society, and cautioned against Denmark drifting in the direction of Nazi Germany.[21] Two years later, he released his first and only film project, *Danmark*, commissioned by the Danish Ministry of Foreign Affairs. It conveyed the image of a radically modern country with footage of wheels, trains and wind turbines. Henningsen's interest in spiralling forms, which would become a key feature in his lighting, was already evident through the circular camera movements around Copenhagen's towers, but the film specifically stood out for its jazz soundtrack, which proved contentious among conservative Danes who would have preferred folk music. It has since been rehabilitated as one of Denmark's most canonical documentaries.[22]

Opposite: Stills from *Danmark* (1935), Henningsen's first and only film project, which depicted modern Denmark through its cityscapes, roads and rural environments, as well as its trains, factories and further sites of industrial progress.

It was the income from the PH lamps that financed Henningsen's other creative pursuits.[23] Louis Poulsen factors into the story in other important ways, too, such as taking out advertising in *Kritisk Revy*. Indeed, the back cover of the third issue of *Kritisk Revy* was a Louis Poulsen advertisement, featuring an inset image of a young boy holding cut-outs of the letters 'P' and 'H' in each hand and looking up at the (glare-free, thanks to its three-shade system) PH lamp above him. The advertising slogan underneath read '1,000 lights in the eyes without blinking'.[24]

Henningsen's entry in the *Dansk Biografisk Leksikon* (*Danish Biographical Lexicon*) states that after *Kritisk Revy*, 'Poul Henningsen stood as his generation's leading cultural critic and the most energetic agitator for a democratic way of life.'[25] After seventeen years as a contributor, he was dismissed from *Politiken* in 1938, when his vocal resistance to Nazism drew the ire of the Danish government, which was leaning into a policy of accommodation and compromise towards Germany. This dismissal significantly limited his opportunities for political expression, and none of the other papers dared to give him column space. Louis Poulsen once again stepped in to help—in 1941, although the company's turnover had more or less ground to a halt because of the war, and in spite of paper shortages, it launched a monthly magazine, *LP Nyt*, with Henningsen as its editor.[26] With the exception of the years 1943–5, when Henningsen had to flee to neutral Sweden (the move likely saved his life, as a Nazi terrorist group was planning to burn down his home)[27], he continued in the role until his death in 1967.

What distinguished *LP Nyt* from most company magazines was the freedom that Henningsen was afforded. While the main topic of the magazine was lighting, Henningsen didn't seem to have an obligation to sing Louis Poulsen's praises. He once published a feature titled 'Ugly things from Louis Poulsen & Co' in which he bemoaned his fellow designers' lack of understanding of lighting theory.[28] He also made no secret of his distaste for fluorescent lights (which he described as only suitable for 'ladies who want to have unsightly hair growth removed'[29]), even though Louis Poulsen produced and sold fluorescent fixtures at the time. More importantly, Henningsen could write about anything that occupied him: architecture and urban planning, of course, but also art, nature and women's rights, and he took advantage of this freedom to make *LP Nyt* the platform for democratic values that *Kritisk Revy* had once been.

Opposite: A Louis Poulsen advertisement for the PH lamp system, published in Henningsen's *Kritisk Revy*. The slogan beneath read '1,000 lights in the eyes without blinking', alluding to the system's glare-free properties.

Nyhavn 11, 28. februar 1943

Grimme Ting fra

˙Det har mindre at sige, om en vittighed er morsom — bare den er plat.

Svend Johansen

Det kan synes en noget mærkværdig ide at begynde at afbilde ting fra firmaet, som tilfældigvis ikke falder i redaktørens smag. Den slags plejer man jo at holde indenfor hjemmets fire vægge. Men for det første har vi forpligtet os til at more læserne efter evne, og mange vil ha erfaret, at de mennesker, som ikke er bange for at la vittigheden gaa ud over sig selv, ikke altid er de kedeligste.

˙ NYT paatænker af og til at bringe berømte nulevende danske mænds ord, og vi starter med hosstaaende af maleren Svend Johansen.

Dette forsøg paa en forbedring af kuglen hedder „Doristankuglen"!

Grimme ting

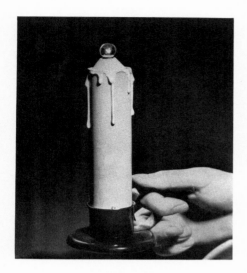

Fotografiet formaar egentlig hverken at gengi det gode eller det grimme. Kuglen paa forrige side er ca 800 gange værre i virkeligheden. Men dette lys taler vel trods gengivelsens slør for sig selv? Det er vist nok beregnet til at gaa rundt med om natten i et sommerhus. Der er altsaa element inden i, og det tændes snildt ved at man skruer paa den lille pære. Er det ikke ganske morsomt, at en fejl ved stearinlyset efterhaanden er blevet til „kunstnerisk motiv"! Dengang man var nødt til at bruge penge kunde en opfinder ha tjent mange penge paa en anordning til undgaaelse af flyderiet. Nedenunder ses en saakaldt A-bordlampe. Ideen er vist nok amerikansk, hvoraf man kan slutte, at de har deres egen lyskultur derovre. Af tændstikæsken fremgaar, at lampen er saa lille, at den ikke lyser nogen steder hen. Naar den har to skærme er det heller ikke af belysningstekniske grunde, men for at der kan flyde lidt „dekorationsbelysning" ud paa den største af dem.

Tilvenstre B- og C-lamper — det er kolossalt rationalistiske betegnelser for en saadan dekorativ opfindsomhed. Lyset er hovedsagelig indirekte, men gennem de lyse felter trænger et svagt gulligt skær ud og forgylder tilværelsen. I baggrunden skimtes dekorative former for kuglebelysninger. Faconen betyder lysteknisk ingenting. Den er skabt af et kunstnersind „for skønhedens skyld"!

Billedet under viser en C-lampet — bruneret metal, gule glas. Man kan ikke læse sin avis ved den.

Det er nemt nok at gøre nar ad andre. Dernæst gør det ikke Louis Poulsen & co. mindre, at ikke alt, hvad de laver, er PHpræget. Det er ogsaa rart for mig, at man ikke gir mig æren for det alt sammen. Og endelig kan denne lille fastelavnsspøg gi anledning til lidt principielle betragtninger over emnet: Hvad er skønhed?

Maaske vil nok et flertal af læserne være enige med mig om, at de ting som afbildes paa de næste sider, ikke er skønhedsaabenbaringer. Men ikke alle. Det er sikkert, at mange vil staa uforstaaende og maaske endda blie lidt stødt over, at nu skal den eller den pæne ting rakkes ned. Titlen paa denne artikel er altsaa forkert. Der skulde staa: Ting, som Poul Henningsen finder grimme. Det er det eneste, der staar fast, og gaar vi ud fra det og forsøger en begrundelse, saa naar vi forhaabentlig til en populær æstetik, en simpel fremstilling af forfatterens kunstneriske livssyn. Hvis det interesserer nogen, kan de læse videre.

Den første ejendommelighed ved billedvalget er, at alle disse ting ganske øjensynlig er formet for at virke smukke. Konstruktøren har gjort sig umage for at det netop skulde blie pænt. Det gælder ikke alle ting, at det træder særlig stærkt frem. For PHlampens vedkommende var udseendet aldeles ikke det vigtigste ved udformnin-

gen. Jeg tør hævde, at det kom i sidste række. Det første og vigtigste var at forme en lampe, som kunde lyse.

Dermed er ikke sagt, at udseendet er en ligegyldig ting. Det interessante er bare, om udseendet springer frem som slutresultatet af en gennemtænkt, rationel og værdifuld konstruktion — eller om man begynder med det.

Man kunde tro, at vi her stod overfor forskellen mellem anvendt og fri kunst. En arkitekt maa først og fremmest lave et hus, man kan bo i. En maler, en billedhugger skal først og fremmest lave noget kønt. Men jeg tror ikke det er saadan. Selv den frie kunstner begynder med noget andet end udseendet.

Efter min mening ligger forskellen mellem god og daarlig kunst i arbejdsmetoden. Et simpelt eksempel er kuglen, som er benyttet saa meget en tid lang til belysning. Lysteknisk set er det naturligvis en meget primitiv løsning, men ogsaa formen er saa klar og simpel, at man kan tale om en kunstnerisk helhed. Naar man stiller belysningsopgaven saa enkelt: lige meget lys til alle sider, nedsat blænding, — ja saa kan det ikke løses smukkere end i én streg, og vi har kuglen. Men saa kommer den næste mand til og finder ud af, at der maa kunne pyntes paa den. Saa laver man kuglen om til en appelsin med indsvajede riller — og det kan ogsaa sælges! Den næste finder paa at skygge rillerne med en orange farve, der driver elegant nedad, og saa er vi naaet til maalet: daarlig kunst. Alle dikkedarerne svarer slet ikke til den primitive belysning, der kommer ud af fyren.

Opposite and above: Excerpts from a 1943 issue of *LP Nyt*, Louis Poulsen's monthly magazine, with a lead article by Henningsen titled 'Ugly things from Louis Poulsen'. 'We have committed ourselves to amusing readers to the best of our ability, and many will know that those who are not afraid to joke about themselves are not always the most boring,' he wrote.

TIVOLI GARDENS

Henningsen's democratic inclinations were further reflected in his tenure as head architect for Tivoli Gardens in Copenhagen from 1940 to 1950, where he played an important role in shaping the world's second-oldest amusement park.[30] With lush gardens, bubble fountains, historicist architecture ranging from a Japanese pagoda to a Moorish food palace, and retail, restaurants and rides galore, Tivoli is already an alluring destination by day, but it truly comes to life at nighttime when it is illuminated with more than 100,000 lights. So magical is the atmosphere here that Walt Disney paid several visits in the early 1950s, in search of inspiration for the first Disneyland.[31] Tivoli remains the most visited attraction in Denmark today.

The park is an unusual success story, considering its very limited footprint of 8 hectares (20 acres)—one-fifth the size of the original Disneyland.[32] It was founded in 1843 by another multihyphenate, Georg Carstensen (1812–57), whose wide-ranging biography has some parallels with that of Henningsen himself. A former officer in the Danish army, Carstensen was inspired by the pleasure gardens that he encountered on travels to various European capitals to propose the creation of an amusement park adjacent to Copenhagen's Central Station, then under construction. He would later use the fortune he amassed from Tivoli to finance various journals and magazines, becoming one of Denmark's press barons;[33] he also collaborated with German architect Karl Gildemeister (1820–69) on the design of the New York Crystal Palace, which hosted the World's Fair of 1853.[34] It would be idealistic to characterize Carstensen as a man of the people—he persuaded King Christian VIII to give him the initial charter for the park by pointing out that 'when the people are amusing themselves, they do not think about politics'.[35] Nonetheless, Tivoli offered an attractive and affordable gathering space at a time when there were few entertaining venues in town, explains Ellen Dahl, a former communications consultant at the park who now works at Copenhagen's Danish Architecture Center: 'From the beginning, all the classes mixed here, and it helped create that sense of equality that we pride ourselves on in Denmark. Everybody pays the same fee at the entrance; everybody has the same right to whatever is on offer. Even though there was a class divide outside Tivoli, on the inside, people from all walks of society would come together, and that still happens today.'[36]

Above: Henningsen inspecting one of his rotating lamps in
Copenhagen's Tivoli Gardens in 1949. The tower of Copenhagen
City Hall is seen in the background.

fr. 12

Ansvarlig redaktør: Poul Henningsen
Udgivet af Louis Poulsen & co. a/s

VALD. PEDERSENS BOGTRYKKERI
KØBENHAVN

This generous spirit would no doubt have drawn Henningsen to the opportunity to work as the park's head architect, in the same year Nazi Germany began its occupation of Denmark (the government surrendered under protest, but discouraged its army and people from resisting). In addition to curfews and rationing, a countrywide blackout order was imposed, requiring all windows to have blackout curtains and all cities to modify their street lamps, to reduce the amount of light emitted and avoid drawing the attention of Allied bombers overhead. Tivoli remained open that year, but only until curfew around dusk.

One of Henningsen's early assignments was to devise a new lamp for Tivoli so that the park could once again remain open until midnight. The park had access to standard-issue blackout lamps, which consisted of an incandescent bulb enclosed in a small white painted capsule. The top of the capsule—marginally larger than the bottom part—reflected light downwards at a 45-degree angle. The problem with this design is that if light fell on a reflecting surface, such as the Tivoli lake or a puddle of water, it would still render the park visible from the air by night. Henningsen's solution was a lamp with ten densely packed layers of horizontal shades. These ensured that light would only be emitted horizontally, illuminating the park and its guests without being reflected upwards.

Upon designing his Black-Out lamp, as it was eventually named, Henningsen had to seek official approval to install it in the park. Initially unconvinced, the authorities relented when they scaled the 105 m (345 foot) tower of Copenhagen City Hall, next door to Tivoli, to confirm that the light from Henningsen's lamp could not be seen from above.[37] In the May 1943 issue of *LP Nyt*, Henningsen reflected on this episode, and expressed his frustration at his design not being implemented more widely: 'People in authority gladly authorize a black-out fitting which does not appear to illuminate but which in the vicinity of water or after rain shines directly up at the sky. But a fitting which shines in the right directions and not the wrong ones is suspicious in advance. We could have had splendid and model black-out lighting in this country. Let us hope that the question never becomes relevant again.'[38]

The Black-Out lamp may have since been consigned to the annals of history, seen only in museum exhibitions (one example is on view at the Danish Architecture Center, within its first permanent exhibition on Danish architecture[39]), but another piece of lighting that Henningsen designed for Tivoli can still be seen at the park today. The Tivoli lamp, as it is called, is instantly recognizable as a Poul Henningsen design and a Louis Poulsen product, but with a dash of whimsy that identifies it as custom-made for an amusement park. The shade— a descending white spiral concealing a single light bulb at its base—was based on his 1942 Spiral lamp for Aarhus University (see page 48) and a transparent acrylic tube in the interior was painted with a red spiral. The shade's internal motor rotated it in the opposite direction of the red spiral, creating a hypnotic effect.[40] Henningsen was specific about the speed of rotation: 'It hit me that a slowly rotating spiral lamp would give a discreet and fine effect. Discretion is important because too much rotation would make people feel drunk! There is also something in the spiral that enhances or anticipates the zig-zag shape of the reflection in the water,' he wrote in the May 1949 issue of *LP Nyt*.[41]

Opposite: Henningsen's 1941–2 Black-Out lamp, designed for Tivoli Gardens in compliance with a nationwide blackout order during the Second World War. This montage from *LP Nyt* shows the lamp switched off (above) and on (below).

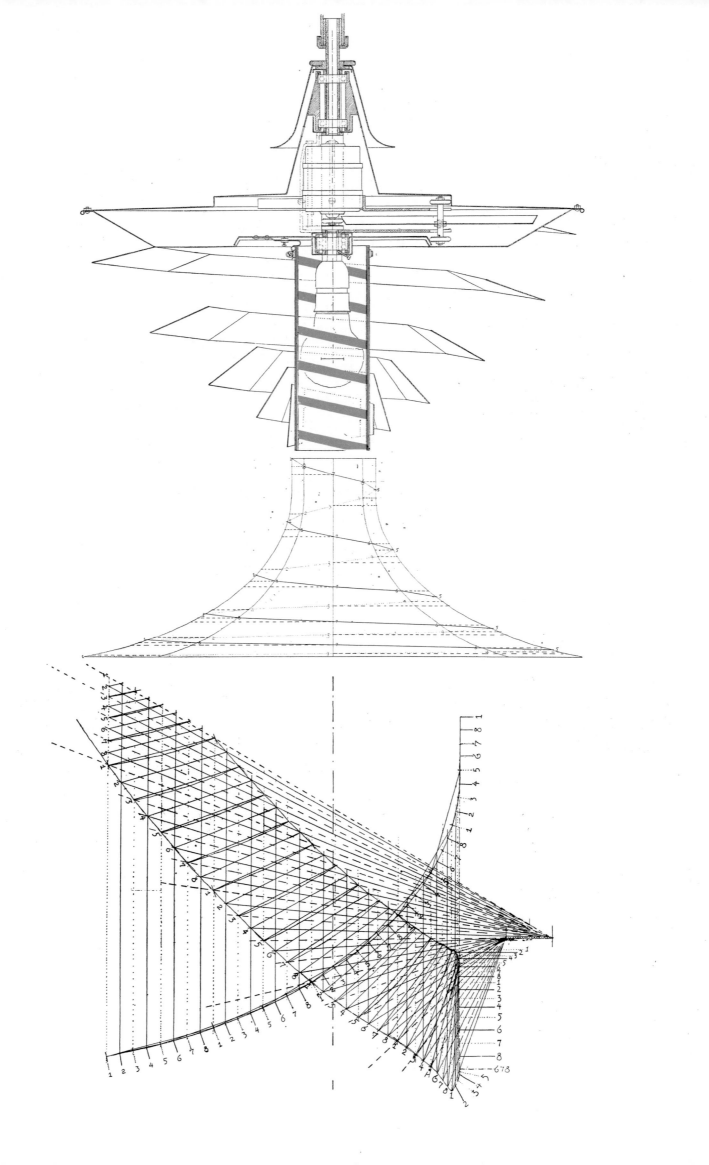

Above: The lamp, with a descending white spiral shade and a transparent acrylic tube in the interior, painted with a red spiral, like a barber's pole. The shade incorporated an internal motor that rotated it in the opposite direction of the spiral.

Opposite: A cross-section drawing of Henningsen's 1949 Tivoli lamp.

　　　　　A Spirit of Democracy

A Spirit of Democracy

The following spring, the Tivoli lamp was installed on cane-shaped poles around the park's lake—some on their own, others in trios at staggered heights. The lamp was a hit, but it soon transpired that the motors were not quite strong enough. Under normal circumstances they could keep the spiral shade in motion, but if something were to get stuck in the shade, such as a stray branch from neighbouring trees, the motor would come to a halt and burn out. There were multiple attempts at improving the motors, but to no avail. Just a few years later, when Henningsen was no longer in the park's employ (the role of head architect went to his son Simon Henningsen, 1920–74), the lamps were left motionless. Happily, in 2008, Louis Poulsen produced a new batch of 101 Tivoli lamps to replace the originals, following Henningsen's design but with a more powerful, Swiss-made motor.[42] These lamps continue to mesmerize the park's visitors today.[43] As a more recent Louis Poulsen collaborator, designer Louise Campbell has commented, 'they bring not only ambience, but also joy'.[44]

Beyond lighting, Henningsen created further designs for Tivoli—thirty-two water vessels for the Parterre Garden, made out of wood due to wartime concrete shortages; a wooden bridge; the Glass Hall, an octagonal, 969-seat auditorium resembling a traditional greenhouse on the outside; and an Open Air Stage for circus shows and musical performances in the shape of a shell, which has since been replaced by a newer building by his son.[45] But his most important legacy at Tivoli is the development plan that he created with landscape architect G. N. Brandt (1878–1945), which divided the park into three distinct zones: a 'traditional Tivoli', including the red-brick entrance gate, Chinese-style Pantomime Theatre and Moorish-inspired palace; a 'park Tivoli' around the lakes, encompassing the gardens, bridges and meandering paths; and a 'popular Tivoli' with rides and other forms of entertainment. The plan remains in place at Tivoli, despite renovations and new attractions over the years, and can be seen as a precursor to the configuration of many subsequent amusement parks around the world.[46]

Opposite left: The Tivoli lake at nighttime, illuminated by Henningsen's rotating lamps.

Opposite right: A 1942 poster for the Tivoli Gardens, drawn by Erik Nordgreen, showing Henningsen's clam-shaped Open Air Stage, which could open and close for circus shows and musical performances.

FURTHER STREET LIGHTING PROJECTS

Louis Poulsen was once again involved when Henningsen returned to the subject of street lighting in 1959 at the invitation of Faaborg, a port town in southern Denmark. This time, as Louis Poulsen's longest-standing and most influential collaborator, he had the full backing of the brand, which committed to financing all his experiments.[47] Despite having designed the Slotsholmen lamp for Copenhagen Energy almost four decades earlier, Henningsen agreed to the commission for two reasons: firstly, lighting technology had grown in leaps and bounds in the intervening period, which was nominally a good thing but also meant that fluorescent tubes had become commonplace. These were much more powerful and energy-efficient than incandescent bulbs, but produced lots of glare. Glare was a persistent source of irritation for Henningsen, but evidently not for many municipal decision-makers. Indeed, at Slotsholmen, the local lighting committee had decided to remove the interior shades within his street lamps, finding them too complicated. 'The result is that people were blinded all the way down the street,' Henningsen described.[48] Happily, Faaborg's lighting committee seemed to share his opinion on glare, and was committed to a non-fluorescent solution for Mellemgade—a street in its old town. It was delighted when Henningsen rose to the challenge, claiming that he could create a different lighting system with the same lighting level and power consumption.

Secondly, Henningsen's views on street lighting had also evolved. It had already dawned on him in the 1930s that street lighting 'like a round pancake' (i.e., where the light would form a circle on the ground surrounding the light source) was only suitable for town squares. He came to believe that when lighting a street, it was better for the light to follow the headlights of cars—a design principle known as 'traffic flow lighting'. While traditional street lighting focused on illuminating horizontal surfaces, it was less effective at highlighting obstructions to cars, such as a jaywalking pedestrian. Indeed, it would sometimes shine in the opposite direction of a car's own directional light, creating a cancelling effect that caused the pedestrian to disappear from view. In Henningsen's view, it was safer for street lights to always point in the direction of the traffic, to better illuminate vertical surfaces that drivers need to avoid.

A Spirit of Democracy

Above: Henningsen at a demonstration of his 'traffic flow lighting' system in summer 1962, on Copenhagen's Strandgade.

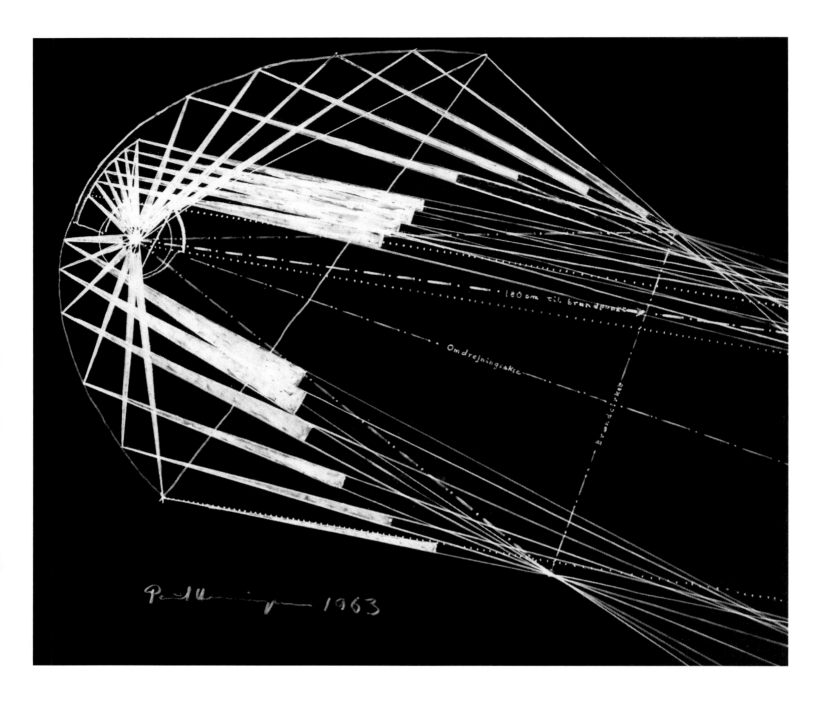

A Spirit of Democracy

There were potential drawbacks to the traffic flow system—it was more effective on wider streets, and had a dazzling effect on cars moving in the opposite direction, which was potentially dangerous for drivers temporarily using the opposite lane to overtake other cars. Nonetheless, most members of Faaborg's lighting committee expressed confidence in Henningsen's experiment when it was implemented in 1960. It was only because of one opponent—a barber who proved persuasive among the press—that the experiment was halted and the town reverted to fluorescent tube fittings.

Henningsen's traffic flow idea was eventually installed in a few places in Denmark and Germany. It never gained the traction he hoped for, nor was he perfectly happy with it. 'The street is lit in clusters! There is still work to do,' he would say in *PH lys*, filmed in 1964.[49] Nonetheless, his ideas continue to have a fair share of admirers, among them designer Christian Flindt, a later Louis Poulsen collaborator: 'I really respect PH for his innovative and broad way of thinking about "good light for the people", no matter where they are,' Flindt says.[50]

Opposite: A 1963 drawing by Henningsen showing how light would be reflected within new street lamps proposed for Copenhagen's Christianshavn.

Above: Henningsen's street lighting system implemented on Copenhagen's Knippelsbrogade. Notice how the light points in the direction of the traffic (Danes drive on the right side of the road).

ONGOING SOCIAL ENGAGEMENT

Given Henningsen's humanitarian approach to design, it is natural that we should ask the question of whether the Louis Poulsen brand has maintained the same democratic spirit in the decades since. On the level of political engagement, the answer is yes, to a limited extent. Emun Rager (1884–1959), the managing director of Louis Poulsen who had given Poul Henningsen the go-ahead to launch *LP Nyt* and use it as a cultural mouthpiece, seemed to share the designer's political views. A trained civil engineer, Rager was a member of the Danish Social Liberal Party (which introduced many welfare reforms in the 1930s and helped build Denmark's welfare state), and served as an MP and Copenhagen city councillor for many years. Rager's successor was Jens Kaastrup-Olsen (1922–76), son of Sophus, who continued to maintain close connections with left-wing cultural, media and political figures in Denmark. Indeed, he once remarked that he would welcome the nationalization of land because it would eliminate detached houses—a somewhat strange position coming from the leader and owner of a major business.[51]

Following Jens Kaastrup-Olsen's death in 1976, Louis Poulsen was listed on the Copenhagen Stock Exchange, and with this the company's radical political tradition also seemed to come to an end. It is normal that a listed company, having to serve the interests of a wide range of shareholders, would be judicious in its political positions. Danish journalist Lars Hedegaard, in his 1999 essay on the company's first 125 years (published in the anniversary issue of *LP Nyt*), offers a complementary explanation, that by the 1960s—the last decade of Henningsen's life—Denmark was rapidly evolving into a more liberal society, and across music, art, social conventions, education, sexuality and other topics, conservative views were fast disappearing. 'In the long run, being a rebel in that sort of society and kicking open doors that are already open becomes a thankless task,' he writes. 'The prudish element had almost been eradicated from Danish society, and the hegemony of the parsimonious agricultural sector had given way to an enlightened urban culture.'[52]

This shift is certainly reflected in the content of *LP Nyt*, which became less political. Which is not to say that the magazine's remit shrank: making up for the loss of social commentary was a wider range of features on how space and lighting inform human wellbeing, no longer restricted to Denmark but rather touching on countries further afield, particularly those where Louis Poulsen lighting was rising in popularity.[53]

Above: Henningsen inspecting one of his PH 5 lamps, as depicted in the 1964 short film *PH lys*. The lamp is estimated to appear in one in five Danish homes.

A Spirit of Democracy

On the level of design output, it is worth examining what it means for a lighting brand to embody democratic values. Cost certainly factors into the equation, but it is not the be all and end all. Henningsen was not averse to creating expensive lighting designs (his PH Artichoke lamp being the prime example), but he was always mindful that price was a key factor in his designs' uptake. In 1962, he fulfilled a long-time dream through the creation of the Contrast lamp, which could emit a cooler light when the bulb is positioned high within the shades, and a warmer light when the bulb is lowered. This entailed an elaborate construction: its ten shades each had four different surface treatments: white painted, blue, red and brightly polished. The painting and lacquer alone called for approximately 130 applications to each lamp. Writing in *LP Nyt* that year, Henningsen apologized that the lamp 'has become bloody expensive […] measured by different standards that is about a fourth of a silver wedding anniversary (and that's not counting the wine)'.[54] In other designs, however, Henningsen did manage to keep costs, and therefore the resulting prices, at reasonable levels. The PH 5 is particularly successful in this respect; according to Signe Lykke Littrup, a curator at the National Museum of Denmark, it appears in one in five Danish homes.[55] Commenting on a 2011/12 retrospective exhibition of Henningsen's lighting at Koldinghus, a castle turned museum in the southern Danish town of Kolding, exhibition manager Axel Johnsen said, 'many people today associate his lamps with exclusivity and a lot of money. But in reality, Poul Henningsen was concerned throughout his life with giving people with limited means access to quality lighting, and thus a better quality of life.'[56]

Post-Henningsen, Louis Poulsen has continued to produce lighting at a wide range of price points. Contemporary additions to the catalogue range from the relatively accessible 2016 Cirque pendant by Clara von Zweigbergk (see page 232) to the 2019 OE Quasi light by Olafur Eliasson, an investment piece that is in any case a bargain for an Eliasson artwork (see page 239). Regardless of the cost, the brand prioritizes the quality of light, appearance, manufacturing and labour conditions. As Monique Faber, the brand's director of product and design, says, 'We do not compromise on quality.'[57] Spare parts are available for purchase, which bolster the overall product's longevity.[58] This is not something one would expect from competitors that might be following the fast-fashion model of manufacturing.

Indeed, in the introduction of *PH lys*, Henningsen had cautioned, 'Do not think that there is such a thing as cheap lighting. People who say that are selling substitutes. It's like selling red wine made from apples and gooseberries.'[59] In this, he seemed to anticipate the British novelist Terry Pratchett's boots theory: 'A man who could afford fifty dollars had a pair of boots that'd still be keeping his feet dry in ten years' time, while a poor man who could only afford cheap boots would have spent a hundred dollars on boots in the same time and would still have wet feet.'[60]

Opposite: Louis Poulsen's Albertslund Maxi Post lamp, designed in 1980 by Jens Møller-Jensen, seen in front of La Grande Arche in Paris. The lamp is an evolution of Henningsen's Slotsholmen lamp and is made from standard components for cost efficiency.

Henningsen's interest in urbanism, with his investigations into street lighting, is certainly borne out by Louis Poulsen's ongoing production of street lamps. The 1963 Albertslund Post by Jens Møller-Jensen (b. 1938) is an evolution of the Slotsholmen lamp, with a reflector ring around the light source to prevent glare. Made from low-cost standard components, the lamp came in at a third of the cost anticipated by the commissioning architects. The first 1,200 lamps were made for a housing development near Copenhagen, which was built by unskilled labour due to the lingering housing shortage in post-war Denmark. Louis Poulsen only charged a nominal fee of 0.5 Danish krone (equivalent to £0.73/US$0.92 today) per lamp for this initial batch, and has continued to produce the lamp for both modern and historic neighbourhoods in Denmark and beyond.[61] So iconic is the Albertslund Post that in 2021, when artist Jeppe Hein (b. 1974) and architect Kristine Jensen (b. 1956) were tasked with creating a wayfinding system that would connect the Arken Museum of Modern Art (now the Arken Museum of Contemporary Art) in Ishøj with the town's train station, a half-hour walk away, they came up with a series of 'dancing street lamps'—reddish orange, with whimsically twirling posts—inspired by Møller-Jensen's design.[62] Complementing the Albertslund Post are more recent street lighting designs by the likes of Alfred Homann, Bystrup Design, Christian Flindt and Mads Odgård (see pages 201, 211 and 229), each catering to a different architectural setting but similarly mindful of the quality of public space.

Louis Poulsen's philanthropic initiatives further attest to the continuation of Henningsen's ethos. For two decades following Henningsen's death in 1967, his widow Inger Henningsen (1904–96) worked with the brand to establish the PH Foundation, which gave an annual prize in support of individuals or organizations that promote developments in architecture, art, theatre, music or the wider social ideals that Poul Henningsen strove for. Its recipients have ranged from the left-wing politician (and later prime minister) Anker Jørgensen; to a campaign against atomic weapons; to an architect working to alleviate drug addiction in Freetown Christiania, Copenhagen; and to the director of the Slaughterhouse Research Institute, to cover legal costs relating to his criticism of Denmark's pig farming industry.[63] Separately, since 2000, Louis Poulsen has run the Sophus Foundation, named after Sophus Kaastrup-Olsen, to support projects that 'promote and improve light quality in a broad sense, including educational, experimental, innovative and artistic initiatives'. In addition to giving an annual grant (renewable for up to three years), the company has also opened its doors to grant recipients, so they can take advantage of its facilities and expertise. Its beneficiaries have conducted material research, proposed lighting solutions for hospitals and historic villages, and gone on study trips to the likes of Florence in Italy and Singapore.[64]

Opposite: Inger and Poul Henningsen at home. The couple met in 1936 and married in 1943. A trained physiotherapist, Inger was nominally Poul's secretary, but also his most frequent interlocutor and most ardent champion. After his death in 1967, she worked with Louis Poulsen to establish the PH Foundation.

COLLABORATING WITH RISING TALENTS

In parallel with the Sophus Foundation, Louis Poulsen has found further outlets for social engagement through one-off collaborations with rising talents. In 2020, Louis Poulsen supported a Copenhagen-based architecture studio, SAGA Space Architects, on a project to develop a lunar habitat. SAGA's co-founders, Sebastian Aristotelis (b. 1994) and Karl-Johan Sørensen (b. 1996), had only recently graduated from the Royal Danish Academy of Fine Arts, but they were backed by experienced scientists and engineers and had an impressive idea for a collapsible, origami-like habitat—with a carbon fibre shell that enabled it to weather extreme conditions, but also a tactile and well-lit interior that a civilian crew would find safe and stimulating. Once LUNARK was built, Aristotelis and Sørensen would bring it to Moriusaq, in far north Greenland (as close to lunar conditions as one could get on Earth), where they would live in complete solitude for sixty days for a behavioural study.[65]

A key challenge of building lunar habitats, or indeed habitats for any extreme environment, is the extreme variation of natural light. During long periods when the sun doesn't rise, artificial lighting becomes a unique source of human wellbeing, explains Marc Fontoynont, a lighting consultant on the project who at the time was a senior researcher at Aalborg University. To simulate daytime, Fontoynont designed seven lighting scenarios (some rich and saturated, others dull and grey) that would play every day on a random basis, with a view of measuring their consequences on a number of activities.[66]

To implement these scenarios, the architects worked with Louis Poulsen and the Long Beach- and Beijing-based LED company Yuji to create a circadian light system within LUNARK, which could simulate changes in sky light around the clock. The system comprised large rectangular panels producing diffused light, which were mounted in LUNARK's ceiling—above the architects' desks, within their sleeping pods and on the airlock. As the module did not have any windows, this 'synthetic sky' became the sole metronome of their lives. 'It gave us an intuitive feel of time passing when the sunlight outside was alien and monotone. Waking up to a sunrise inside our sleeping pods was an incredible natural feeling,' Aristotelis would later recall.[67] This impression of sunlight helped remind the body that it was daytime, and accordingly meant that when night fell, the architects' natural instincts would kick in to help them sleep.

As the circadian light panels dimmed in the evenings, the architects would turn to their Louis Poulsen Panthella lamps—a portable version following a 1971 design by Verner Panton (see page 169)—to make their space more dynamic. 'Turning on the Panthella lights sort of had the same effect of lighting a candle in the evening. It was really such an atmosphere creator. We're trying to make it *hyggelig* while still trying to make it work as an engineered habitat,' remembers Sørensen.[68] Functional and beautiful as they are, it is unclear whether Panthella lamps would be suited for usage on the moon.

Opposite: SAGA Space Architects' LUNARK in Moriusaq, far north Greenland, where founders Sebastian Aristotelis and Karl-Johan Sørensen spent sixty days for a behavioural study.

On a broader level, it is worth examining the value of this project for Louis Poulsen. Given the more recent billionaire space race, and the astronomical spending and carbon footprint it entails, there has been a fair amount of criticism volleyed at space exploration altogether—as doubters would say, why invest in lunar expeditions when we should be focusing our efforts on improving our own planet? To this, it might be countered that the learnings from a mock lunar expedition can contribute new insights into how the extreme corners of the Earth can be made more hospitable, which is certainly a worthy cause. It can also demonstrate the way architects—so integral to Louis Poulsen's past and future—can move beyond traditional disciplinary boundaries and play a bigger role in confronting the existential threat of the climate emergency. With its century's worth of expertise in good light, Louis Poulsen can make contributions to scientific research, which in turn will help the brand and its design collaborators refine their humanistic approach to design.

Kasper Hammer, erstwhile director of product and design for the architectural and outdoor category at Louis Poulsen, says of the collaboration with SAGA, 'We wanted to tell the story that regardless of how fast technology develops, the way our eyes and brain function, the way we react to light, doesn't change very quickly. We still perceive light exactly the same way we have for thousands of years. We have natural light, and we have fire. That's how we build our designs.'[69]

Louis Poulsen should further take pride in having supported an emerging architecture studio on a project that has elicited an enthusiastic response: following the 2020 expedition, SAGA Space Architects has presented solo exhibitions on LUNARK at the Danish Architecture Center and at Aalborg's Utzon Center[70], as well as creating the Denmark and Switzerland Pavilion at the 2023 London Design Biennale.[71]

Opposite: The interior of SAGA Space Architects' LUNARK, featuring nendo's NJP table lamp and Verner Panton's Panthella 160 Portable lamp, both by Louis Poulsen.

A Spirit of Democracy

Above: Lise Vester's *Fabrikkens Idea Generator* installation, on view at Copenhagen's Fabrikken for Kunst og Design, as part of the 2022 Cabinetmakers' Autumn Exhibition. It is 90 cm (35½ inches) tall and 180 cm (71 inches) in diameter.

DESIGNING FOR HUMAN WELLBEING

In another wise investment in the next generation, Louis Poulsen collaborated with Copenhagen-based designer Lise Vester (b. 1991) on a light installation in October 2022. The occasion was the Cabinetmakers' Autumn Exhibition, an annual show of contemporary and experimental furniture designs that are notable for their technical, functional and artistic qualities.

A graduate of London's Royal College of Art, Vester had just established her studio that year, following her belief—inspired by a collaboration with a Danish hospice where her aunt had spent her last days in 2011—that design and architecture can enhance health and mental wellness, by creating environments that stimulate, care for and support people through different stages of life.[72] 'Designing with empathy for people's needs, is how I hope to contribute with design to improve our wellbeing,' she says.[73]

The exhibition took place at Copenhagen's Fabrikken for Kunst og Design (Factory for Art and Design), Denmark's largest studio building, which houses just over seventy-five local and international visual artists and designers within its forty-eight studios and 1,000 sq m (10,800 sq foot) production hall. Inspired by the bustling creativity of this venue, Vester came up with the idea for her *Fabrikkens Idea Generator* installation, formed from forty-eight neon tubes, each emitting a soft, baby blue glow that symbolizes the bright spark facilitated by each of Fabrikken's studios. The handcrafted tubes, shaped like C hooks, totalled 60 m (197 feet) in length and were laid out in a circular configuration to form a chandelier that appeared symmetrical from all angles. 'With the chandelier I wanted to challenge the typical neon sign aesthetics and create a three-dimensional object that makes the experience of atmospheric light spacious because of the form and scale of the design,' she explains.[74]

Less than a year since it initially went on view, *Fabrikkens Idea Generator* has already made a marked difference in Vester's burgeoning career: in November 2022, she was named Designer of the Year by Danish interior design magazine *Bo Bedre* (the judges applauded her work for epitomizing 'innovation and hope'[75]), and her chandelier was on view in the library lounge of Designmuseum Denmark until late 2023—a sound affirmation of her design approach, as well as Louis Poulsen's role in empowering creativity in the service of human wellbeing.

The PH Artichoke

LANGELINIE PAVILION

The PH Artichoke lamp, which Poul Henningsen created in 1958, is easily his crowning achievement. Initially designed for Langelinie Pavilion, an upmarket restaurant and social hub overlooking Copenhagen harbour, with a view of the famous Little Mermaid sculpture, the PH Artichoke has since been used the world over. It is a staple of museum collections (besides the Designmuseum Danmark, it has been collected by the Museum of Modern Art, New York, the Victoria and Albert Museum in the UK and the Vitra Design Museum in Germany)[1] and design books, and one of two cover stars of *Danish Lights—1920 to Now*, the definitive volume on Danish lighting design.[2] In 1998, *Wallpaper** magazine included the PH Artichoke in a 'Hall of Fame' of six legendary designs that epitomize contemporary style, alongside the leather sofa designed by American architect and designer Florence Knoll (1917–2019) and the 606 Universal Shelving System by German designer Dieter Rams (b. 1932),[3] while two decades later, *Architectural Digest* described it as having 'changed the trajectory of lighting design'.[4] The lamp even features prominently in the office of Prime Minister Birgitte Nyborg, protagonist of the popular political drama TV series *Borgen*.[5] So it would be no exaggeration to call the PH Artichoke the most iconic product by Louis Poulsen, which has kept it in constant production in the decades since.

The story of the PH Artichoke began in 1957, when architects Nils Koppel (1914–2009) and Eva Koppel (1916–2006)—partners in life and work—won a public competition to build a new Langelinie Pavilion to replace the one that had been destroyed during the Second World War. They proposed a cantilevered, high-ceilinged glass box in the International Style, with a recessed upper level, all atop a reinforced concrete base. This design beat entries from other leading Danish architects including Jørn Utzon (1918–2008), who envisioned a pagoda-inspired glass tower with ten floors, and Henning Larsen (1925–2013).[6] Charged with creating both the building as well as its interior, the Koppels turned to Henningsen for the lighting design. Nils Koppel would later recall of the commission that they admired Henningsen's 'honest view of lighting, which perfectly unites with his unique artistic and humorous abilities'.[7]

The Koppels came up with five criteria. Firstly, they needed a chandelier that could be used throughout the U-shaped public area, which, depending on the day, would be used in its entirety or divided into a restaurant and private dining rooms. Secondly, the design should take into account the architectural style of the building. Thirdly, the chandeliers would need to be supplemented by table lamps and wall fixtures. Fourthly and most importantly, the chandeliers should be 'festive and emanate a warm glow'. And finally, they should be decorative and appealing even during daytime, when they are switched off.[8]

Opposite: Poul Henningsen's 1958 PH Artichoke lamp in its intended setting—the Langelinie Pavilion in Copenhagen, designed by architects Nils and Eva Koppel to replace a previous pavilion that had been destroyed during the Second World War.

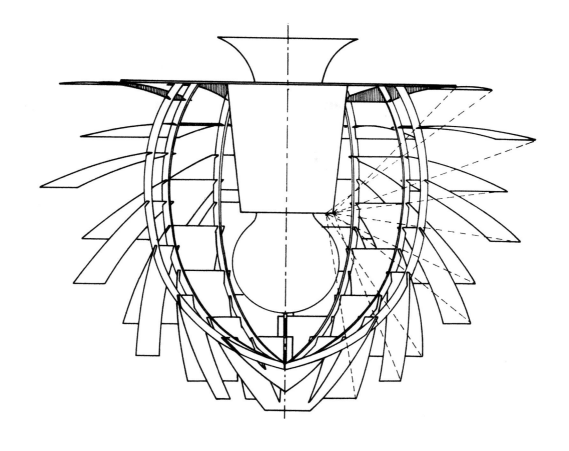

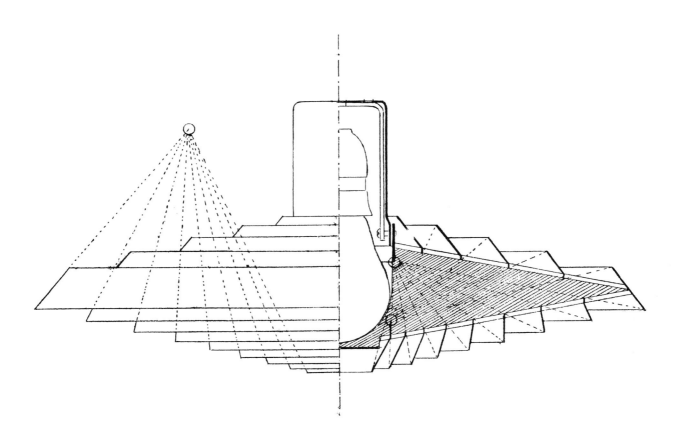

Opposite, above: The Langelinie Pavilion during lunch service in 1959. The PH Artichoke lamps are complemented by PH Plate lamps closer to the curtains, also designed by Henningsen. Opposite, below: The PH Plate lamp was also installed as a wall fixture at Langelinie.

Above: Cross-section drawings of the PH Artichoke and PH Plate lamps.

THE PH ARTICHOKE'S ROOTS

Considering the resulting design's complexity, it is remarkable that Henningsen came up with it in just three months. Indeed, he only made rough sketches before the lamp was physically installed at Langelinie.[9] He was drawing on more than three decades of experience in lighting design, however, and specifically, revisiting ideas that he had explored in an earlier lamp called the PH Septima, developed between 1927 and 1931. As its name suggests, the PH Septima has seven shades. All have the same curvature, but the top, fourth and sixth shades follow the form of a PH lamp (specifically in size 5/5), while the others are sized accordingly to create the lamp's tapering proportions. All of these are made out of clear glass, treated so that it has alternating clear and frosted stripes radiating from the centre of each shade. When assembled, the shades are positioned on top of each other so that the frosted stripes cover the clear stripes underneath, to better diffuse the light and minimize glare. The PH Septima was a hit as soon as it was shown as a prototype at the Danish Museum of Decorative Art (now the Designmuseum Danmark) in 1928, and the white original was followed by variations with amber, pale rose and light blue shades (the pale rose and blue PH Septimas were completely frosted, with their stripes achieved via enamelling). Its warm critical reception was no surprise—while more decorative than the original PH lamp, with a mesmerizing glow that invited viewing from various angles, it still bore the hallmarks of a Henningsen design and could direct light rays effectively. But it had shortcomings too: with seven layers of glass, the lamp could not be shipped in its finished form and rather had to be assembled on site, ideally by an electrician. It also had to be taken apart and reassembled whenever the light bulb had to be changed, a regular occurrence in an era of incandescent bulbs. Thus, the PH Septima was phased out in 1940 due to wartime material shortages.[10] It was only reintroduced to Louis Poulsen's catalogue in 2020, this time with Italian borosilicate glass for added strength, and an improved suspension system.[11]

Opposite, above and below: Louis Poulsen campaign images from 2020 show the newly reissued PH Septima.

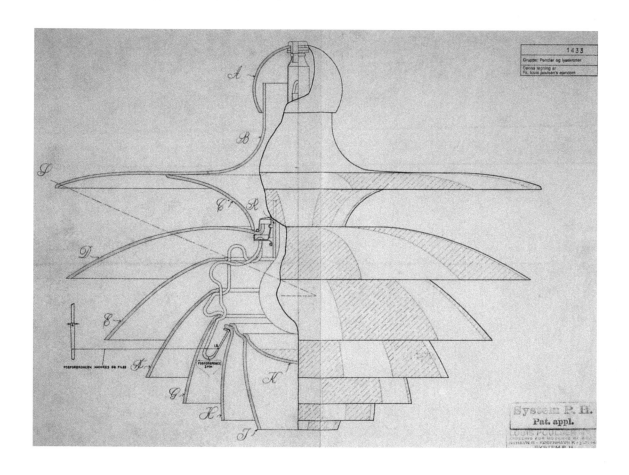

In developing the PH Artichoke, Henningsen turned to old, unrealized drawings of a metal version of the PH Septima, which had seven staggered layers of trapezoidal metal leaves where the frosted glass stripes would have been, and left empty the spaces originally filled by clear glass stripes. He evolved the design to have twelve layers, each with six metal leaves, mounted on a nickel-painted brass frame. To properly direct the light, and achieve the PH Artichoke's biophilic form, the leaves in each layer had to be shaped and bent differently— the widest and flattest at the top, and the narrowest and curviest at the bottom to cradle the light source.[12] Like the leaves of an actual artichoke, the layers were staggered: it was 'made as a type of louvre with six shades', but the staggered design 'gives more play and richness and it splits the mental impression comfortably with division into twelve times six leaves instead of six rings,' Henningsen wrote in the April 1958 issue of *LP Nyt*.[13] The placement of the leaves also ensured that the light source is never directly visible, and the light is directed at oblique angles in all directions.

Opposite: The original PH Septima in white, with alternating clear and frosted stripes radiating from the centre of each shade. Frosted stripes always cover clear stripes underneath in order to better diffuse the light and minimize glare.

Above: An original sketch of the PH Septima, featuring a cross-section of its seven shades on the left.

The PH Artichoke

Henningsen used copper leaves for his original design. These were lightly brushed and lacquered on the outside, and coated with a reflective layer of pale pink paint on the inside, so as to achieve a rosier glow that would complement the skin tones of the Langelinie Pavilion's guests. Nils Koppel would later express his pleasure with the result: 'when you look over the rooms in the evening, the Artichoke lamp dominates and creates a festive light [...] and when you sit at one of the tables, they cast their gentle, golden, embellishing light on patrons and tables.'[14]

It is worth pointing out that for all its functional and aesthetic qualities, the PH Artichoke is an atypical Henningsen design that seems to contradict his long-held democratic ideals. The different shapes of the twelve layers of leaves made the manufacturing process extremely complex (today, the leaves arrive at Louis Poulsen's factory in Vejen already laser-cut, but are sanded down and polished using custom machinery developed in the 1970s. The factory also has an abundance of twelve-drawer storage units, better to separate leaves intended for different layers).[15] The amount of material used for the leaves also complicates the task of hanging the lamp: the originals at Langelinie were so heavy that they had to be suspended with steel aircraft cables.[16] 'The Artichoke is not classless in any meaning of the word,' writes design historian Mark Mussari in *Danish Modern: Between Art and Design*. 'It is an ultra-expensive designer creation, a striking accomplishment, but worlds removed from Henningsen's social design contentions.'[17] This said, it is worth considering that for Henningsen, the PH Artichoke was a late-career design, completed in his mid-sixties. By then, he had already created an extensive catalogue of more accessible lighting, and the Danish economy was in a period of unprecedented growth (per capita GDP increased 4.5 per cent annually throughout the 1960s). A little opulence did not seem out of order. Henningsen was certainly proud of the PH Artichoke, highlighting it in various international exhibitions such as the Danish pavilion at the 1960 Triennale di Milano, where it was displayed alongside a sofa by Poul Kjærholm (1929–80), a candle by Søren Georg Jensen (1917–82) and a carpet by Vibeke Klint (1927–2019).[18]

Above: The PH Artichoke at the headquarters of Scripps-Howard Newspapers—the 1962 Pan Am Building (now known as the MetLife Building) in Manhattan, New York.

Above: The PH Artichoke in polished steel, hanging at The QVEST
hotel in Cologne, Germany.

The PH Artichoke

THE PH ARTICHOKE'S LEGACY

Like most classic lighting and furniture designs, the PH Artichoke has been issued in new variations over the years: for instance, with matte white rather than pink paint on the interior of the copper leaves, as white is the most reflective colour (all things being equal, a lamp with white shades would give a brighter light than its coloured counterparts). The lamp was only produced in copper in Henningsen's lifetime, but an all-white PH Artichoke was launched in the 1980s, and a stainless steel version in the 1990s.[19] For the lamp's fiftieth anniversary in 2008, Louis Poulsen unveiled two more extravagant commemorative editions: one in frosted glass,[20] and the other in copper but plated with 24-carat gold.[21] The glass version, which is still in production, has an ice-like appearance that recalls the PH Artichoke's roots in the PH Septima lamp, although its effect is to diffuse light like a glowing orb rather than to direct it downwards—so opinions differ as to whether Henningsen would have approved. The fragility of the glass leaves means that, like the original PH Septima, the glass PH Artichoke has to be assembled in situ by a specialist—who in some cases may have to be flown halfway across the world, compounding the cost of the product.[22] Nonetheless, there is no denying that this offering has enhanced the mythical qualities of the PH Artichoke.

The gold-plated version, meanwhile, proved problematic, not least because of the material's ostentatious connotations, which seemed too much of a contradiction of Denmark's contemporary value system.[23] The unfortunate timing of its release—just days before global financial markets crashed—meant that the few initial orders were quickly cancelled by buyers who suddenly found themselves short on cash. A now-retired member of the Louis Poulsen team believes that if you searched the brand's factory in Vejen thoroughly, you may still come across the gold-plated PH Artichoke leaves that have never been mounted. It is appropriate that recent issues have adhered to a more modest material palette: Louis Poulsen launched a brass version in 2018,[24] a black one in 2020[25] and a 'pale rose' one in 2023,[26] with the same pale rose finish throughout as the interior of the original PH Artichoke.

Alongside material variations were variations in size. Henningsen had designed the PH Artichoke in three sizes, with diameters of 840 (the version installed at Langelinie Pavilion), 720 and 600 mm (33, 28 and 24 inches) respectively. The 2006 release of a smaller version, with a diameter of 480 mm (19 inches) was an ingenious decision that expanded the PH Artichoke's popularity. Suited to lower-ceilinged spaces, this variation meant that quite a few people who previously could only admire the PH Artichoke in public areas could now have one at home.[27] Indeed, as British journalist Patrick Kingsley wrote in the 2012 book *How to Be Danish*, 'I have lost count of the number of houses that have a Poul Henningsen Artichoke lamp hanging from the ceiling.'[28] Abroad, the PH Artichoke remains beloved among the design cognoscenti: Noritsugu Oda, Japan's leading authority on Scandinavian design, has one in his living room in Hokkaido;[29] Junichi Abe, founder and designer of fashion label Kolor, likewise keeps one in his Tokyo living and dining room;[30] while Nina Yashar, founder of the celebrated design gallery Nilufar, has one in her Milan kitchen.[31]

Above: A Louis Poulsen campaign image from 2020, showing the newly launched black version of the PH Artichoke in four sizes.

Opposite: A campaign image from 2023 showing the new pale rose PH Artichoke, with copper leaves painted in the same hue that Henningsen had initially specified for the innerside of the leaves.

The PH Artichoke

It is also worth noting that the PH Artichoke was initially named the PH Kogle—*kogle* meaning 'pine cone' in Danish. The name was translated into 'Zapfen' in German, 'Pomme de pin' in French and 'Kotte' in Swedish. Indeed, the shaping of the lamp's leaves more closely resembles the radiating scales of a pine cone rather than the more enclosed form of the artichoke, and while pine cones are commonplace in Scandinavia, artichokes are native to the Mediterranean and would have been somewhat limited in availability in Henningsen's Denmark. According to the Dutch design historian Thimo Te Duits, the lamp has mainly only been known as the Artichoke since the 1970s, above all in the English-speaking world.[32] Today, the name 'PH Artichoke' is used worldwide, including in Japanese translation.

It is testament to the PH Artichoke's popularity that despite multiple changes of ownership at Langelinie Pavilion, and multiple interior renovations—most recently in 2018, led by local furniture brand &Tradition[33]—Henningsen's PH Artichoke remains an integral part of the decor. Remarkably, when a pack of thieves broke into Langelinie in 2009, it was the lamps that had caught their eye—cutting the suspension cables, they stole the five original lamps and attempted to sell them on eBay, only to be thwarted by the police.[34] In the years since, the original lamps have been sold at auction,[35] so the ones on site today are more recent Louis Poulsen productions.

Fittingly, the PH Artichoke remains an inspiration to contemporary designers. In a 2018 interview, designer Louise Campbell recalled, 'what has probably given me the greatest pleasure is the sight of the PH Artichoke in copper. At my college, there were rows of them hanging high up from the ceiling in the large assembly hall where we often had to sit, and where—for one reason or another—you often found yourself leaning back and gazing upwards. Its inherent beauty had and still has a calming effect on me.'[36]

Opposite: A close-up of the original PH Artichoke at Langelinie Pavilion. Its copper leaves were lightly brushed and lacquered on the outside, and coated with a reflective layer of pale pink paint on the inside, to achieve a rosier glow that would complement the skin tones of Langelinie Pavilion's guests.

The Cradle of Modernism

ARNE JACOBSEN

Arne Jacobsen (1902–71) is perhaps the most influential architect in Danish history, credited for introducing modern architecture to the country in the 1930s. While championing the International Style, he was also mindful of craft traditions and material qualities, paving the way for the contemporary Danish approach to architecture. Within his home country, his extensive portfolio includes a series of buildings (sea bath, housing estate and cinema) in Klampenborg, Aarhus City Hall, the SAS Royal Hotel in Copenhagen and the Danmarks Nationalbank, also in the capital. Among his buildings abroad are St Catherine's College, Oxford, the Danish Embassy in London, both in the UK; and Mainz City Hall in Germany; and if it weren't for his fear of flying, he would likely have made a big impact on American architecture too.[1]

Jacobsen's interest in Gesamtkunst (total works of art) and remarkable eye for detail led him to create many lighting, furniture and accessory designs that, while mostly intended for specific projects, were soon put into wider production and still remain available. Given his stature, it is no surprise that any brand in possession of the production rights of his designs—of which there are fifteen today[2]—would wear this as a badge of pride. But Louis Poulsen has a greater claim than most, based on its decades-long collaboration with the architect, which began in 1929, the same year he set up his own practice. In 1927, as a recent graduate of the Royal Danish Academy of Fine Arts, Jacobsen teamed up with another young architect, Flemming Lassen (1902–84), to enter a competition to design the House of the Future. Their winning proposal, which had a circular layout, white-plastered exterior walls and futuristic technical solutions, referenced both the Bauhaus and the work of Le Corbusier.[3] Two years later, when a 1:1 model of their House of the Future was built for the Housing and Building Exhibition at Copenhagen's Forum, Jacobsen would design a floor lamp for it, produced by Louis Poulsen. This brass lamp, which came to be known as the AJ Reading lamp, had a flat base, a pliable hose neck and a curved conical shade that was painted white, cut off at a 45-degree angle to create a bigger field of light. It was one of the architect's earliest design projects to be put into production.[4] Although it wasn't a runaway success (and wound up being discontinued by Louis Poulsen in 1970), it set an important foundation for Jacobsen's later, more popular lighting designs.

Opposite: The stairs of the lobby of the Danmarks Nationalbank designed by Arne Jacobsen in 1971, featuring the 1955 Munkegaard lamps made by Louis Poulsen.

Above: A 1:1 model of Jacobsen and Flemming Lassen's House of the Future, exhibited for the first time at Copenhagen's Forum in 1929.

Opposite: The interior of Mainz City Hall in Germany by Jacobsen and Otto Weitling (b. 1930), his studio partner from the mid-1960s. The building was designed in 1968 and completed in 1973. Notice the use of Louis Poulsen AJ Wall lamps.

The Cradle of Modernism

Jacobsen continued to work with Louis Poulsen over the years. In 1933, paint dealer A. Stelling commissioned the architect to create the Stellings Hus on a corner of Gammeltorv, the oldest square in Copenhagen. He designed a six-storey building with a rounded corner, housing an art supply shop on the ground and first floors, and offices in three storeys above, and a penthouse apartment. Full-height windows were installed on the ground and first floors, while the rest of the building was clad in grey-blue ceramic tiles, punctuated with square windows.[5] On this occasion, he worked with Louis Poulsen to make an opal glass pendant lamp hung on piano wire, and a brass desk lamp (which would also be installed in at least two other Jacobsen projects—a Copenhagen office for Landmandsbanken, and Søllerød Town Hall, which was co-designed by Flemming Lassen), and both remained in the brand's catalogue for a number of years.[6]

Opposite: A street view of Jacobsen's 1937 Stellings Hus at the corner of Gammeltorv, the oldest square in Copenhagen.

Above: A shop window at Stellings Hus, featuring opal glass lamps hung on piano wire, and brass desk lamps, both designed for the project and made by Louis Poulsen.

Louis Poulsen's collaboration with the architect continued throughout the 1930s with the Søllerød pendant, an opal glass globe made for the aforementioned town hall;[7] and the HIK bracket lamp for the tennis hall at Hellerup Athletic Club,[8] in which Jacobsen also specified Henningsen's Tennis lamps (see page 64). However, Jacobsen's most successful product with Louis Poulsen, the AJ lamp, would not arrive until 1957. The year before, Jacobsen was enlisted by Scandinavian Airlines to design the SAS Royal Hotel, across from Copenhagen Central Station. The twenty-two-storey building comprised an air terminal on the ground and first floors (when it came time for boarding, passengers would be whisked by shuttle bus directly to their plane, waiting at Copenhagen Airport about a twenty-minute ride away) and hotel rooms in the glass tower above. Not only was it Denmark's first skyscraper, it also symbolized the country's new-found prosperity and international outlook. Jacobsen was given free rein to create every detail of the hotel. For this, he introduced many designs that have since achieved international renown in their own right, including the AJ lamp (available in floor, table and wall variations), the AJ pendant, the Egg chair and the Swan chair.[9] The first two were produced by Louis Poulsen, where they remain integral to the brand's catalogue today.

Opposite: Søllerød Town Hall (known today as Rudersdal Town Hall), completed by Jacobsen and Lassen in 1942.

Above: The entrance hall at Søllerød Town Hall, featuring the custom-designed opal glass Søllerød pendant, made by Louis Poulsen.

Top and above: The Panorama Salon and lobby of Jacobsen's SAS Royal Hotel, Copenhagen, completed in 1960, respectively featuring the AJ Royal pendant lamp and AJ Wall lamp.

Opposite: The architect in front of the twenty-two-storey hotel, about 1960. The building remained the tallest skyscraper in Denmark until 1969.

The Cradle of Modernism

The AJ lamp stands out from Jacobsen's earlier lighting designs because of its strict geometric form: the shade comprises an oblique cone and a cylindrical tube that conceals the socket. The upper side of the cone flows seamlessly into the cylinder, while the base of the cone is parallel to the horizontal surface the light falls on. The floor and table versions—the latter coming in two sizes— are supported by a slender metal stem, set at an angle from a slanted base with a circular aperture, while the wall version connects simply to a circular mount. The lamp's combination of straight and oblique angles not only mimicked those of Jacobsen's Series 3300 sofas and lounge chairs (launched prior to the SAS Royal Hotel, but made famous by its inclusion in the Air Terminal), but also aligned with the striking geometric profile of the building.[10] Initially produced in light grey, dark brown and black, the lamp is a perennial bestseller and is now available in nine colourways.[11]

Above, right: A 2023 campaign image showing the reissued AJ Table in warm sand. Above, left: A 2020 campaign image showing the reissued AJ Table lamp in chrome, with the same finish as the original lamps that appeared at the SAS Royal Hotel, which celebrated its sixtieth anniversary that year.

Opposite: A Louis Poulsen campaign image from 2023 showing the AJ Floor and AJ Oxford in black.

Meanwhile, the AJ pendant (now renamed the AJ Royal) has a dome-shaped shade, 500 mm (20 inches) in diameter with six horizontal slits near its top, in order to produce an ambient upwards light and a stronger but even downwards light, and a frosted acrylic diffuser at its base. A 370 mm (14½ inch) version, without the acrylic diffuser, was designed a few years later for St Catherine's College at Oxford (see below). Like the AJ lamp, the AJ pendant was produced in light grey, dark brown and black.[12] The colour selection has since been narrowed down to white and black, but to mark the sixtieth anniversary of the hotel in 2020, a smaller variant (250 mm/10 inches) was introduced,[13] which opened up more applications for this timeless design.

Besides the AJ lamp and AJ pendant, Louis Poulsen also has in its catalogue the 1955 Munkegaard lamp, a recessed fixture initially designed for the Munkegaard School in Gentofte[14]; the 1956 AJ Eklipta wall and ceiling lamp, designed for Rødovre Town Hall[15]; and the 1964 AJ Oxford table lamp, for St Catherine's College.[16] The latest was first installed in the college's dining hall, an impressive, 350-seat space with exposed brick walls, concrete pillars and beams, and clerestory windows. Its lengthy oak tables—lined with long wooden benches (since replaced with Series 7 chairs) for students, and high-backed Oxford chairs for fellows—have pin-mounted AJ Oxford table lamps as their centrepieces.[17] The table lamps are notable for their biconvex shades—each with a metallic upper half, and a lower half made of mouth-blown opal glass to give a soft, harmonious light. These connect to a dark brown metal element that conceals the socket, supported on a slim stem (elsewhere in the college, where the lamp is not pin-mounted, the stem coils into a circle to form the base). Louis Poulsen had discontinued the AJ Oxford in 1971, but reintroduced it in 2023. 'We worked closely with the Arne Jacobsen Design company and [Jacobsen's grandson] Tobias to make this design available again. It is the ideal complement to our existing product assortment, and it builds on the story of a close and fruitful relationship between Arne Jacobsen and our brand,' explains Monique Faber, the brand's director of product and design. Unlike the AJ lamp, which is sculptural and geometric, the AJ Oxford is a softer alternative, ideal for building islands of light at home.[18]

Opposite: The AJ Royal pendant in black, as featured in a Louis Poulsen campaign image from 2020.

Above: A classroom at Jacobsen's 1957 Munkegaard School in Gentofte, featuring the 1955 Munkegaard fixture, made by Louis Poulsen.

Opposite: The Munkegaard lamp installed at the offices of Kopenhagen Fur. The uppermost level features Vilhelm Wohlert's 1959 Satellit pendant, also for Louis Poulsen, now marketed as the Wolhert pendant.

The Cradle of Modernism

Above: The 1959 AJ Eklipta lamp, designed for Rødovre Town Hall and intended for both the indoors and outdoors.

Opposite: The 1964 AJ Oxford table lamp, as seen in a Louis Poulsen campaign image from 2023, when the lamp was reintroduced into the brand's catalogue.

Opposite: The dining hall at St. Catherine's College, Oxford, UK, in the 1960s, when the tables were lined with benches rather than Jacobsen's Series 7 chairs.

Above: A 2012 photograph of the dining hall, with the AJ Oxford table lamp (custom-made by Louis Poulsen) built into the long oak tables.

VILHELM LAURITZEN

Another leading modernist architect who enjoyed a prolific, multi-decade collaboration with Louis Poulsen was Vilhelm Lauritzen (1894–1984). Eight years older than Arne Jacobsen, he began his career at a time when architecture was more focused on form and ornamentation, and played a pivotal role in introducing simpler, functionalist architecture to the Danish public. He is best known for having designed the original terminal at Copenhagen Airport—commissioned in 1936, at the dawn of commercial air travel, it pioneered the division of airport terminals into airside and landside sections, which is still followed by most airports today. His other important buildings include the Radio House (Radiohus) in Frederiksberg, combining sound studios, a concert hall and administration offices for the Danish Broadcasting Corporation (today, the building is home to the Royal Danish Academy of Music), the People's House (Folkets Hus) in Copenhagen, a cultural complex with a theatre stage, cinema and banqueting room (now known as VEGA—The House of Music), and the Danish Embassy in Washington DC. Although he had little interest in personal fame and preferred to stay behind the camera,[19] he remains a household name in Denmark, and the architecture practice that bears his name continues to flourish with high-profile projects both at home and abroad.

Lauritzen was consistently mindful of both daylight and artificial lighting. Within his buildings, he would balance out north- and east-facing windows with south- and west-facing ones, so as to merge warmer and cooler light. His light fixtures invoked the same idea, combining directed and diffuse light to create the desired ambience.[20] In 1954, he would describe his lamp design criteria as follows in *LP Nyt*: 'It should be easy to clean, not gather dust at the base, not shatter with the first knock, offer simple bulb replacement, minimize glare (without adjustments) and be available for downward as well as evenly distributed light, as needed. And it should look nice.'[21]

Many of these principles were already evident in Lauritzen's 1929 Universal pendant, manufactured by Louis Poulsen and shown the same year at the International Exposition in Barcelona, Spain (see page 263), where the company staged a full presentation of PH lamps. The two-part shade comprised a cone—with a top part in chrome-plated metal and a wide rim in opal glass—and an opal glass hemisphere to conceal the bulb, creating a downward light with a diffused glow in all directions.[22]

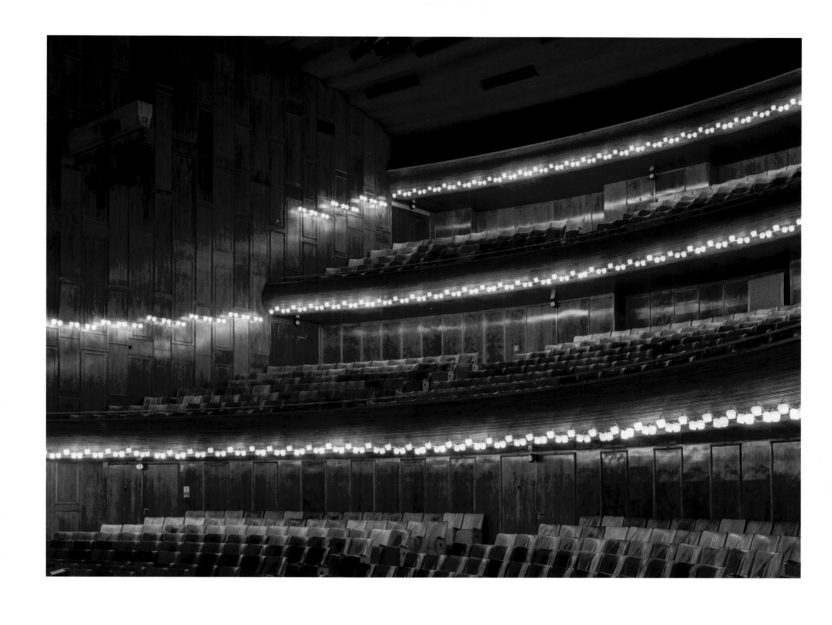

Above: The 1,058-seat concert hall at Vilhelm Lauritzen's Radio House in Frederiksberg, opened in 1945, is entirely lined with wood. It features oxhide upholstered seats and small lamps with clear references to lily of the valley.

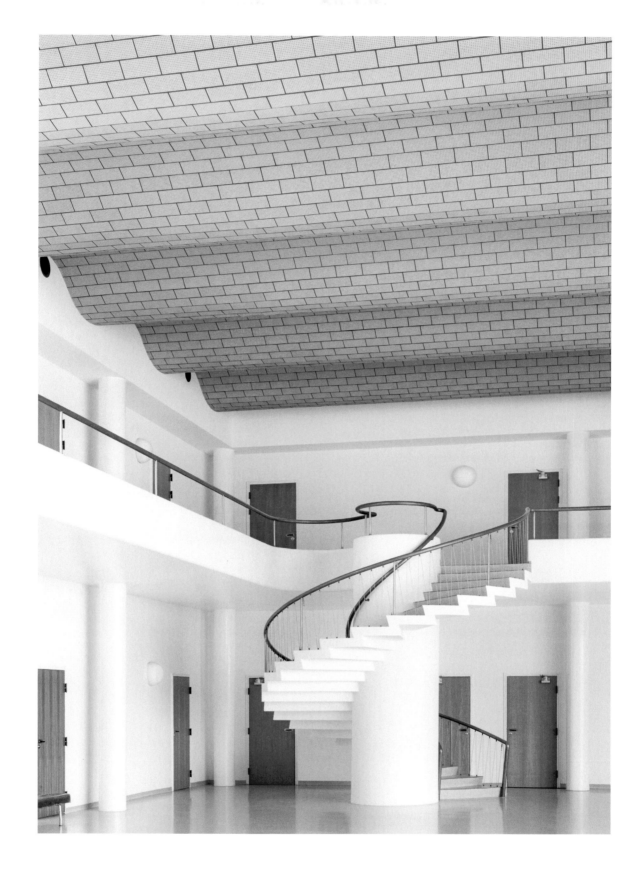

Opposite, above: Lauritzen's 1929 Universal pendant at the International Exposition in Barcelona, Spain, that same year, where it was awarded a gold medal. Opposite, below: A sketch of the Universal pendant.

Above: The main hall at the original terminal at Copenhagen Airport, completed by Vilhelm Lauritzen in 1939.

The Cradle of Modernism

Opposite: An original drawing of the facade of Lauritzen's People's House, with a three-storey-high relief by artist Dan Sterup-Hansen (1918-95).

Above: A 1956 photograph of the big hall at the People's House (renamed VEGA—The House of Music in 1996).

Lauritzen's best-known lamps were created in dialogue with Mogens Voltelen (1908–95), who worked for him from 1937 to 1947. Many of them were created for the Radio House, whose opulence reflects the central role that radio played in Danish society in the 1930s (construction ran from 1936 to 1942, but the building remained closed until September 1945 because of the war). Exclusive materials were used throughout the building—Lauritzen specified mahogany for interior cladding, oxhide for the 1,058 auditorium seats and the ceiling of the foyer, and Greenlandic marble for the facades.[23] Needless to say, the lighting also had to be of the highest quality. Among the custom designs was the VL45 Radiohus pendant, with a brass suspension and a singular mouth-blown opal glass shade in the form of a vertically compressed capsule. A circular void at the bottom of the shade means the light there is slightly brighter,[24] accentuating the lamp's sculptural qualities. Then there was the VL38 table lamp, whose white metal shade is shaped like a matryoshka doll, cut at an oblique angle to achieve a more dynamic appearance and complemented with a brass stem.[25] There was also the VL Studio, a globe-shaped wall lamp comprising a brass upper hemisphere and a opal glass lower hemisphere, initially used outside studios to indicate whether recording was taking place (a red light would indicate that recording was in progress, while a green light showed that the studio was free to enter).[26] Interestingly, Lauritzen's lamps for the Radio House were released to the public in 1941, even before the Radio House opened, and the VL45 Radiohus pendant in particular became a bestseller.[27] They were taken out of production over the years,[28] but reintroduced between 2016 and 2022,[29] suggesting a resurgence of interest in Lauritzen's work and anticipating the one hundredth anniversary of Vilhelm Lauritzen Architects in 2022.

Opposite: Lauritzen's VL45 Radiohus pendant, reintroduced into Louis Poulsen's catalogue in 2016 and photographed at the Radio House, for which it was initially designed. Underneath is the VLA75 Foyer bench, also by the architect.

The Cradle of Modernism

Opposite, Lauritzen's VL Studio, a globe-shaped lamp initially used outside recording studios to indicate whether recording was taking place, reissued by Louis Poulsen in wall and floor versions in 2021.

Above: Lauritzen's VL38 wall lamp, reissued by Louis Poulsen in 2016, at the Radio House.

Another notable lamp by Lauritzen, the VL Ring Crown, was designed for the Radio House but never installed there. This, too, had an opal glass shade shaped like a matryoshka doll, but with a horizontal cut at the bottom so the shade could be used in clusters—ranging from three to twenty-four—to form chandeliers. The design was popularized in 1947, when designer Finn Juhl (1912–89), who had worked at Lauritzen's studio between 1934 and 1945,[30] used VL Ring Crown chandeliers in his showroom design for porcelain brand Bing & Grøndahl (a predecessor of Royal Copenhagen) in central Copenhagen. It has thus been referred to as the B&G pendant. Lauritzen would eventually use the shade design for a series of chandeliers at Christiansborg Palace, which he installed in 1951.[31] Some of these chandeliers still hang at Christiansborg today.

Lauritzen's collaboration with Louis Poulsen continued through the 1950s—for instance, with the 1956 Guldpendel and Sølvpendel pendants, designed for the People's House. The respective brass and chrome-plated aluminium shades—roughly cylindrical, with rounded corners—each had a hollow bottom, surrounded by eight rings of perforations. This was a playful way of directing the light downwards while gently diffusing it at an oblique angle. A less obvious, but no less thoughtful innovation was the tube at the top of the shade, which concealed a winding device so that the cable can be shortened and let out as required.[32] The designs were reintroduced as the VL 56 pendant in 2023, albeit without the winding device.[33]

Throughout his career, Lauritzen insisted that architecture should serve the general public, rather than being the privilege of the few, which brought his views in line with those of Poul Henningsen. Their relationship was one of mutual admiration, although they did not always agree: Henningsen found the material palette of the Radio House too opulent, and pointed out that oxhide should be used for shoe leather, not for sticking on ceilings. Lauritzen countered that oxhide would age more gracefully than paint.[34] Henningsen also complained about Lauritzen's affinity for custom lighting: 'the tendency to want to design everything from scratch each time is unfortunate and makes construction expensive,' the designer wrote in a 1951 issue of *LP Nyt*.[35] Given Lauritzen's track record of custom designs finding broader applications, it would seem that the architect has the last word.

Above: Although designed for the Radio House, the VL Ring Crown lamp (seen in the building's boardroom in this contemporary photograph) was not installed there until a recent renovation.

Above: The VL 56 pendant (originally named Guldpendel/
Sølvpendel, depending on its material), designed by Lauritzen in
1956, installed along the perimeter of a room at the Radio House.   Opposite: The VL 56 pendant was reissued by Louis Poulsen in 2023.

The Cradle of Modernism

Above: Architects Vilhelm Wolhert and Jørgen Bo in 1958, in front
of the brick wall outside what was initially the library of the Louisiana
Museum of Modern Art, Humlebæk, Denmark.

The Cradle of Modernism

OTHER MID-CENTURY DESIGNERS

Although Henningsen, Jacobsen and Lauritzen dominate the story of Louis Poulsen in the mid-twentieth century, the brand also worked with many other key figures of the modernist movement. It was Louis Poulsen that first produced Finnish designer Alvar Aalto's Golden Bell pendant in 1937, for his Savoy restaurant in central Helsinki. As the name suggests, the pendant is made of polished brass, with a streamlined bell shape. A ring of vertical slits near the bottom of the shade diffuses a small amount of light downwards.[36] Although Aalto had founded his own brand, Artek, two years earlier, it made sense that he would seek out Louis Poulsen for this project as he had used PH lamps for many of his projects by that point and drawn inspiration from Henningsen for his own lighting designs. It is also indicative of Louis Poulsen's increasingly global reach by the 1930s.

Another striking design was the MK 114 Double Cone pendant by architect Mogens Koch (1898–1992), which was created in 1956 for the extension of the Royal Veterinary and Agricultural University in Frederiksberg, Denmark. The shade is formed of two truncated cones, placed back-to-back so it resembles an hourglass in silhouette, albeit with a larger lower cone. The joint and screws that connect the two cones are left deliberately visible, adding to its industrial look and feel, which relates to the lamp's original purpose of illuminating the university's laboratories.[37]

When architects Vilhelm Wohlert (1920–2007) and Jørgen Bo (1919–99) were commissioned in the mid-1950s to build the Louisiana Museum of Modern Art in Humlebæk, Denmark, they turned to Louis Poulsen to create a custom pendant. Designed by Wohlert, the 1958 Louisiana pendant had a hemispherical shade, available in copper and brass versions, with a white interior and concentric white metallic louvres inset at its base to reduce glare. In this, Wohlert, who had studied lighting design under Lauritzen's colleague Mogens Voltelen at the Royal Danish Academy of Fine Arts, drew inspiration from the old lamps at the Academy's sculpture studio. The Louisiana lamp was produced in three diameters: 300, 450 and 600 mm (12, 18 and 24 inches), and used in two ways: within the galleries, it was installed high up and at an angle to highlight the artworks on the walls, while in the library and café it was suspended vertically.[38] The lamp was also sold at the museum shop, albeit with nylon grating replacing the metallic louvres,[39] which is likely a reflection of the amount typical museum-goers were willing to spend on souvenirs. Wohlert continued to work with Louis Poulsen for many decades. One of his opal glass lamps, called the Satellit (now marketed as the Wohlert pendant), remains in the catalogue.[40]

Opposite, above: The Louisiana pendant, installed at an angle in Louisiana Museum of Modern Art's Lantern Gallery, with paintings by Vilhelm Lundstrøm (1893-1950) and Harald Leth (1899-1986). Opposite, below: The Louisiana pendant in the museum's Lake Gallery, originally known as the Larsen Stevns Room.

Above: The Satellit pendant, as featured in the Louis Poulsen catalogue in 1968. The lamp is now marketed as the Wolhert pendant.

The Cradle of Modernism

Sculptor and painter Henning Koppel (1918–81) is best remembered for his long-standing collaboration with the Georg Jensen company, creating silver hollow-ware, flatware and jewellery with abstract yet sensuous forms.[41] Lesser known are his lighting designs for Louis Poulsen, including the 1962 Petronella and the 1972 Bubi. Today, we may raise our eyebrows at the fact that the Petronella, released seven decades after electricity first arrived in Denmark, was powered by kerosene. But even amid the growing prosperity of the 1960s, some Danish households still didn't have electricity. It was Anker Tiedemann, the founding editor-in-chief of interior design magazine *Bo Bedre*, who lamented to Louis Poulsen's managing director Jens Kaastrup-Olsen that there weren't any modern kerosene lamps. At Tiedemann's suggestion, Kaastrup-Olsen approached Koppel to create one.[42]

With its graceful curves, the opal glass shade of the Petronella lamp bears a close resemblance to a minimalist vase that Koppel had created for Georg Jensen in the 1950s (this was produced in pewter back in the day; today, it is available in mirror polished stainless steel),[43] although the brass base, where the wick is embedded, has a more voluptuous form. Completing the design is a clear glass chimney, which connects the two elements and protrudes from the top of the opal glass shade. The name 'Petronella' is likely a reference to the Danish word for kerosene (*petroleum*) and a Catholic saint, considered the daughter of the apostle Peter and possessed of extraordinary beauty. Advertisements for the lamp emphasized its enduring light ('50 hours of light on a single drink of kerosene'), and its portability,[44] which made it suitable for balconies, patios and gardens. The Petronella was discontinued in the early 1990s, but one can imagine that, with advances in battery technology and the growing popularity of portable lamps today, it might be due for a reissue in modernized form.

While the Petronella was meant to evoke a woman, the Bubi was inspired by a young boy, specifically Koppel's grandson Adam, wearing a narrow-rimmed sun hat, although it might be clearer to compare the Bubi to a sleigh bell, with the top half and ridge made from brass and the bottom half made from white polycarbonate. The choice of polycarbonate rather than opal glass made the design less fragile, as Koppel envisioned that it could either be used as a pendant or simply lie on the shelf.[45] Alas, being only 130 mm (5 inches) high and 190 mm (7½ inches) in diameter, the Bubi was prone to overheating and discontinued just a few years later. As design dealer Murray Moss wrote in his book on Georg Jensen, Koppel 'was neither interested nor professionally invested in the functional performance of the objects he designed'[46]—it seems that this description of Koppel's silver designs would ring true for the Bubi too.

Opposite: Henning Koppel's Bubi lamp, as featured in the Louis Poulsen catalogue in 1972, the year it was introduced.

Louis Poulsen also had a fruitful relationship with Hans J. Wegner (1914–2007), which may come as a surprise given the designer's reputation as a master of chair design. Before he set up his own studio in 1943, Wegner worked for Arne Jacobsen and Erik Møller (1909–2002), Jacobsen's then collaborator, and was tasked with creating all the custom furnishings for Aarhus City Hall—including the lighting, which was produced by Louis Poulsen.[47] It would be two decades until he would create Louis Poulsen designs under his own name: the 1962 Wegner pendant, which had a large aluminium shade intersecting a quadrant-shaped handle that had an integrated mechanism for adjusting the position of the light source within the shade.[48]

In the 1970s, Wegner was asked to design the interiors for Hotel Scandinavia in Copenhagen, which would become the largest hotel in Scandinavia on its completion in 1973. This resulted in the Opala collection, comprising table lamp, floor lamps and pendants, all characterized by conical shades in opal acrylic (much sturdier than glass) with rounded caps in lacquered metal. Frustratingly, the hotel manager quickly rejected Wegner's design as too modern, and insisted on more conventional lamps with porcelain bases and fabric shades instead. Louis Poulsen nonetheless put the Opala lamps into production a few years later, to coincide with its production of Wegner's street light—the result of a competition organized by the brand for lighting in architectural heritage settings.[49] Within the street light, the light source points upwards at a tilted reflector disc, so the light is directed at the road and does not disturb the inhabitants of nearby buildings.[50] With minor modifications, such a design could have suited Henningsen's principle of traffic flow lighting—one imagines the master of light would have approved.

Above: Hans J. Wegner's 1962 Wegner pendant, whose handle
had an integrated mechanism for adjusting the position of the light
source within the shade, as featured in the Louis Poulsen catalogue
in 1968.

Above: Verner Panton's 1971 Panthella floor lamp is characterized by
its harmonious, calm form. The semi-circular shade creates a soft,
pleasant light. ©Verner Panton Design AG.

VERNER PANTON

As a young designer and architect, Verner Panton (1926–98) was steeped in the Danish design establishment—he wed Henningsen's stepdaughter Tove Kemp (1928–2006) in 1950, and although the marriage did not last, Henningsen became his close friend and mentor. Henningsen encouraged the younger man to further his investigations of light theory and develop new principles for light design to better disperse light. It was also Henningsen who organized the dinner where Panton first met Arne Jacobsen, who would employ the younger designer from 1950 to 1952. Panton was part of the team that designed Jacobsen's iconic Ant chair, the first industrially made chair in Denmark. The project affirmed his interest in industrial manufacturing and material innovation; Panton would later say that he never learned as much from anyone as he did from Jacobsen.[51]

Looking at Panton's first lighting designs, which he presented at the annual exhibition of the National Association of Danish Crafts in 1955, we can clearly see the influence of his forefathers—each of the nine pendant lamp designs comprised ring-shaped reflecting shades, held in geometric formation by wires, and a single-coloured shade above and around the light source. (The lamps were later purchased by a restaurant at Tivoli, which used them for a few years.[52]) Within a few years' time, however, Panton's designs would diverge significantly from the Danish modernist mainstream, embracing a dynamic colour palette, playful shapes and material innovation. In a nation that prized neutral tones, elegant minimalism and natural materials, Panton's futuristic output proved polarizing—he felt his design approach differed from that of contemporaries such as Finn Juhl and Wegner.[53] So, in 1963, he moved to Switzerland, where he found a kindred spirit in Willi Fehlbaum (1914–2003), the founder of Swiss furniture company Vitra,[54] which produces many of his furniture designs to this day. This is not to say that he turned his back on Denmark—he continued to collaborate with various Danish design brands, among them Louis Poulsen, which he ushered into a new era of fluid, dynamic and colourful design.

The Cradle of Modernism

Panton's first project with Louis Poulsen was the 1959 Topan lamp, a relatively simple design involving a spherical shade with the lower section removed so the light could shine through. What made the lamp stand out was its polished aluminium finish (more daring variants in blue, turquoise, orange or red lacquer launched in 1967). The lamp was made famous in 1960 by its inclusion in Panton's design of the Hotel Astoria in Trondheim, Norway, where he used the polished aluminium version: each room was a riot of red, orange or purple, filled with Op art fabrics and populated with Cone swivel chairs that Panton designed, in both wire-framed and heart-shaped variants. Unlike anything that Scandinavia had seen at the time, the Astoria was a visual overdose, but not at the expense of functionality. As Henningsen commented, the restaurant 'is a square peg in a round hole. It's something else, because it combines the stubbornness to stick to an idea with due regard for the guests' comfort.'[55]

Opposite: Panton's 1960 Visor pendant (which Louis Poulsen marketed in 1961 as the Moon pendant), with ten individually adjustable lacquered aluminium rings mounted on a vertical axis. ©Verner Panton Design AG.

Above: Panton's 1959 Topan lamp in the café of Hotel Astoria in Trondheim, Norway, for which Panton created the interiors the following year. ©Verner Panton Design AG.

Panton's interest in kinetic art is evident in the 1960 Visor pendant (which Louis Poulsen marketed the next year as the Moon pendant, perhaps capitalizing on the widespread interest in lunar exploration during the Space Race). The design involves ten lacquered aluminium rings, nested into one another and mounted on a vertical axis, which allows each ring to be swivelled independently. The rings hide the light source and at the same time serve as reflectors, diffusing a soft light throughout the room, which can be adjusted simply by tweaking the rings' configuration.[56] Its playful nature aside, this pendant is also notable for the way it packs down. It can be shipped in assembled form but laid flat, with all its rings on the same plane,[57] which made the design well ahead of its time.

Panton's big and lasting sales success would come in 1967 with his Flowerpot lamp, which had two hemispherical metal shades facing one another, the diameter of the upper shade twice that of the lower one. The lower hemisphere shields the bulb, so all the light would bounce off the interior of the upper hemisphere to provide downward illumination. The exteriors of both shades were either polished steel or enamelled in turquoise, white, red or orange, and the electric wires were also coloured to match. The lamp was easy to make, and Danes bought it in droves (more than 240,000 small Flowerpots were sold in 1968 alone).[58]

Another feature that distinguished the Flowerpot was its ability to be grouped into clusters to form a chandelier.[59] Panton first did this in an exhibition commissioned by the German pharmaceutical company Bayer, which took place on a ship floating on the Rhine in Cologne; more famously, he would set up 'chandeliers' of Flowerpots throughout his canteen design for German magazine *Der Spiegel*,[60] part of a wider commission to redo the company's headquarters in Hamburg. What started with an uninspiring brief ('the interior must provide an impression of serious and dignity [...] it should avoid any character of fashion') wound up becoming one of the most memorable corporate interiors of the twentieth century, awash in vibrant colours from floor to ceiling, with different palettes for the editorial offices, administrative offices and conference rooms.[61] All textiles, wall claddings and lamps were Panton's own, and to illuminate the walls he also created bespoke fittings with Louis Poulsen—square panels of stamped iron that look as though they have Flowerpot lamps embedded into their surface—which the brand would eventually put into wider production as the Spiegel lamp.[62]

Above: A 1969 photograph of the canteen at the headquarters
of German magazine *Der Spiegel*, with interiors by Panton, featuring
'chandeliers' comprised of Flowerpot lamps. ©Verner Panton
Design AG.

Første tryk på knappen gir 60 watt
(almindeligt lys)

Andet tryk på knappen gir 100 watt
(altmuliglys)

Tredie tryk på knappen gir 160 watt
(ualmindelig altmuliglys)

Fjerde tryk på knappen - slukker
(Det er ganske enkelt)

Panton once again used a hemispherical shade on his 1971 Panthella table and floor lamp, this time made of polycarbonate. What distinguished the Panthella was its base, flared at its top and bottom.[63] The flaring gives the design an organic appearance rarely seen in modernist lamp designs. Depending on your point of view, it either makes the overall form reminiscent of a toadstool or lends it a Space Age quality. But the form also served a functional purpose, helping to diffuse the light across its space.

Another important innovation within the Panthella was its four-step switch. Paired with a specially designed two-filament bulb, the switch could not only turn the light on and off, but also increase its brightness. A Louis Poulsen advertisement, which was printed on four consecutive right-hand pages in a 1971 issue of *LP Nyt*, showed a Panthella table lamp and Panthella floor lamp side by side, against a black background. They increased in brightness across the first three pages, making the portrait of Panton behind them more legible as they did so, and then disappeared into the darkness on the fourth page. The text on the respective pages read, 'First press of the switch gives 60 watts (ordinary light) // Next press of the switch gives 100 watts (all-purpose light) // Third press of the switch gives 160 watts (extra-strength all-purpose light) // Fourth press of the switch—turns off (It's quite simple)'.[64] It was a witty way of communicating the lamp's properties that no doubt drew inspiration from Panton's maverick character.

Opposite: An advertisement for Panton's Panthella lamp, printed on four consecutive right-hand pages in a 1971 issue of *LP Nyt*, showing a Panthella table lamp and a Panthella floor lamp with increasing degrees of brightness and finally switched off. A photograph of the designer appears in the background. ©Verner Panton Design AG.

The 1970 Ilumesa demonstrates Panton's exceptional ability to persuade manufacturers to stretch their capabilities. This was not just a floor lamp, but also a side table (advertisements also showed a female model using the Ilumesa as an ottoman, although its lack of padding would have made it rather uncomfortable for sitting). Twice as wide as it is tall, the Ilumesa is made of two almost identical cylindrical sections, one on top of the other, with the lower section containing an upright fitting for a light source. With this design, which could be used both indoors and outdoors, Panton wanted to disrupt traditional furniture typologies and encourage social interaction. 'Nowhere is it written into law that a living room must forever be furnished with a sofa and two easy chairs around a low table. There must be other, perhaps better, approaches to a home environment dedicated to relaxation and leisure,' he explained in *LP Nyt*.[65]

Above: The Fritz Hansen and Louis Poulsen exhibition at the furniture fair, Bella Center, Copenhagen, 1972. The products exhibited include the Panthella floor lamp, Flowerpot and Spion (spy) lamp. ©Verner Panton Design AG.

Opposite: The Panthella 250 table lamp on the left with Panthella 160 Portables on the right. The latter were released in close collaboration with the Panton family in 2021, are Louis Poulsen's first battery-powered portable lamps.

Panton's collaboration with Louis Poulsen lasted until 1998, when he worked with the brand on ten dodecahedral light sculptures for his retrospective exhibition at the Trapholt Museum for Modern Art and Design in Kolding (sadly, the designer died just two weeks before the exhibition's opening).[66] He created many groundbreaking products in his time. Alas, the Panthella is the only one that remains in Louis Poulsen's catalogue; others became casualties to evolving tastes. As sales dwindled, they were phased out over the years to make way for new launches by a younger generation of designers, and the relevant licensing agreements have lapsed.[67] This is not itself an indictment of Panton's abilities, but rather a reflection of where Louis Poulsen's priorities lay. Panton created designs that resonated in an era of individual expression, that tapped into the latest technologies and stretched what was industrially possible, and proposed new ways of living. He introduced vivid colour and expressive forms into a design culture that was wary of both, and blurred the boundaries between sculpture and design.

The Henningsen connection may have played a role in persuading Louis Poulsen to produce his Topan pendant back in 1959, but the longevity of the subsequent partnership is entirely down to Panton's merits, and the brand's eagerness to champion a fresh and exciting vision. It is also worth noting that many discontinued lighting designs have been brought back by other companies in the past two decades, a sure sign of the cyclical nature of tastes. For its part, Louis Poulsen has been stewarding Panton's legacy carefully. The designer had initially envisioned a version of the Panthella lamp with a chromed metal shade and base, but that had to be discontinued early on due to technical difficulties.[68] Louis Poulsen has now resolved these difficulties and sells a chromed metal version based on Panton's original design. And the tech-savvy Panton would no doubt have been pleased with the Panthella 160 Portable, released in close collaboration with the Verner Panton family in 2021, which is not only Louis Poulsen's first battery-powered portable lamp, but also retains the four-step dimming system as he had intended.[69]

Opposite: Verner Panton with Inger and Poul Henningsen and Percy von Halling-Koch in 1960. Panton had wed Inger's daughter Tove Kemp in 1950, and although the marriage did not last, Henningsen remained his close friend and mentor. ©Verner Panton Design AG.

173

Craft and Technology

Above: Henningsen with his PH 5, PH Artichoke and PH Plate lamps,
all launched in 1958.

FROM INCANDESCENT BULBS TO LEDS

The tale of the Louis Poulsen brand is also a tale of technological progress: relaunched as a dealer of lighting and electrical supplies in 1892, just as Copenhagen's first power plant opened its doors, the company has evolved its product range over the years in response to development in lighting technology—first and foremost the popularization of the incandescent light bulb, which offered a cleaner, more convenient and more enduring alternative to traditional candles and kerosene lamps.

The incandescent light bulb is a glass bulb encasing a wire filament, which heats up and glows as an electric current passes through it. Various forms of the bulb were developed in the mid-nineteenth century, although the invention year is often given as 1879, when American inventor Thomas Edison (1847–1931) applied for a patent of an 'electric-lamp' that 'gives light by incandescence' through 'a light-giving body of carbon wire or sheets coiled or arranged to such a manner as to offer great resistance to the passage of the electric current' (the patent was granted in 1880).[1] What distinguished Edison's invention from previous attempts was that he successfully created a vacuum within the glass bulb, which prevented the build-up of by-products and made the filament last longer.[2] This carbon filament bulb would be mass-produced until the 1920s,[3] when it was outsold by more powerful tungsten filament bulbs, patented in 1913.[4]

Increasingly powerful lighting levels meant more glare—by Poul Henningsen's calculations, if the glare from a candle was set at 1, the glare from a kerosene lamp would be 1.5, a gaslight would be 8, the carbon filament bulb 120, and the metal filament bulb 300. His point was that it fell on the lighting designer to rein back the glare: 'to be hygienic, modern light must generate considerably less glare than candlelight', he wrote.[5] His dislike of glare may also have been fuelled by his mother Agnes, who complained that the harsh light from electric bulbs revealed her wrinkles.[6] It is worth noting that not everyone at the time saw glare as a problem: for some, a powerful light that could effectively turn night into day was an emblem of innovation. As architecture historian Sandy Isenstadt describes in *Electric Light: An Architectural History*, some homeowners 'sought glare as an unprecedented and thrilling visual experience, they longed to surrender to the luminous spectacle as if optical discomfort were itself a register of material progress'.[7] (Henningsen would criticize this blind pursuit of brightness in the 1964 short film *PH lys*: 'The technician has an old dream of turning night into day. I think that dream is wrong and lacks creativity. We need the rhythm of day and night. I wouldn't want night to become day.'[8])

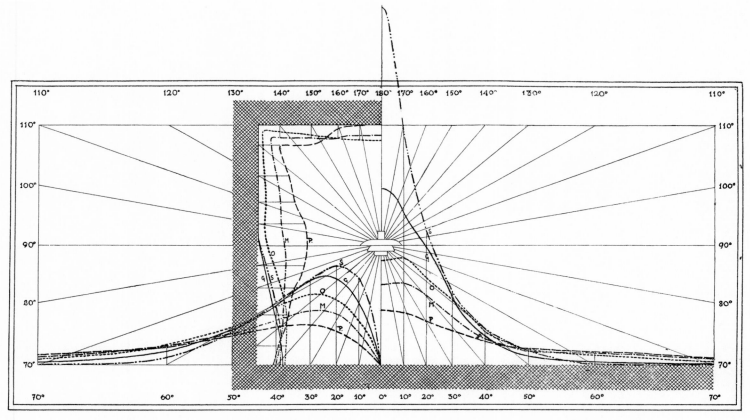

Diagram over Lysfordelingen fra forskellige **P H** Lamper paa vandrette og lodrette Flader i Rummet.

A willingness to overlook, and perhaps even embrace, optical discomfort certainly helps explain the lighting fixtures that had been popular in Denmark before the rise of the PH lamp: fabric shades, often with fringes and other decorative elements, which blended the modern incandescent bulb into a traditional domestic interior but did little to reduce glare.[9] In parallel, there were opal glass fixtures that essentially consisted of placing glass domes around incandescent bulbs[10]—which diffused the light and thus reduced glare, but ultimately was uneconomical in that the light would shine with equal strength in all directions. What made the PH lamp revolutionary was its ability to provide glare-free illumination directed at the surfaces that needed it most—thus properly harnessing the power of the incandescent bulb while minimizing its deleterious effects.

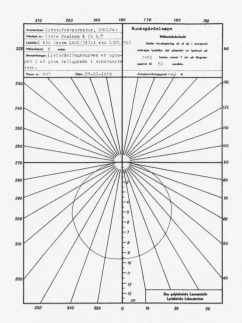

Munkegårdslampe 280L243 for 1x40 watt og 1x32 watt cirkulære lysrør. 1 deling svarer til 15 candela ved en lysstrøm på 1000 lm. Armaturvirkningsgrad 42%.

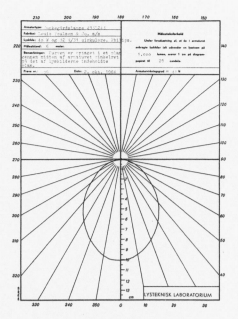

Munkegårdslampe 483L243 for 1x40 watt og 1x32 watt cirkulære lysrør. 1 deling svarer til 28 candela ved en lysstrøm på 1000 lm. Armaturvirkningsgrad 48%.

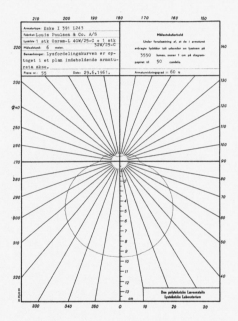

Eske I 391L243 for 1x40 watt og 1x32 watt cirkulære lysrør. 1 deling svarer til 14 candela ved en lysstrøm på 1000 lm. Armaturvirkningsgrad 60%.

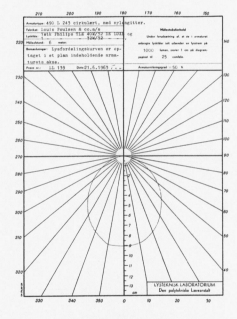

Cirkus 490L243 for 1x40 watt og 1x32 watt cirkulære lysrør. 1 deling svarer til 25 candela ved en lysstrøm på 1000 lm. Armaturvirkningsgrad 50%.

Opposite: A light distribution diagram from a 1927 Louis Poulsen catalogue, showing how a three-shade lamp diffuses light on the vertical and horizontal surfaces of a room.

Above: Light distribution curves for various Louis Poulsen lamps, including the Munkegaard (in two sizes), Eske I and Cirkus lamps.

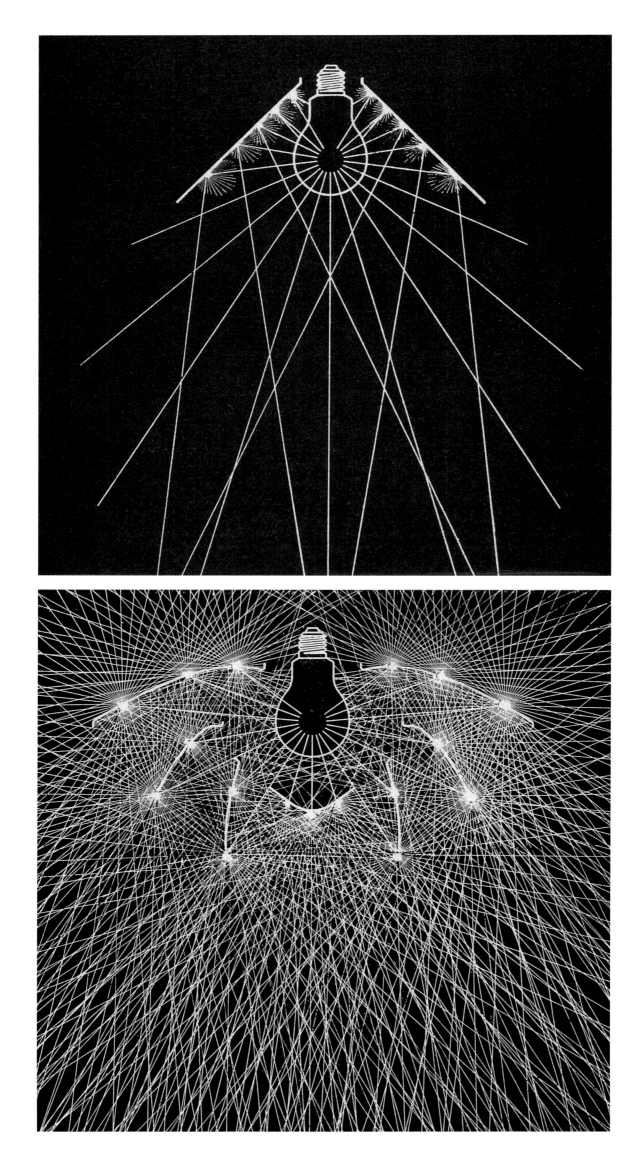

The introduction of the PH 5 lamp in 1958, three decades after the original PH (see page 31), likewise responded to a recent technological development: increasingly, bulb manufacturers were enclosing filaments in frosted rather than clear glass, which meant that light emanated from the entire bulb surface rather than just the single filament—this had the effect of weakening glare, but at the same time made it more difficult to shield the light source from direct view. The PH 5 solved this problem with its internal shades, which enclosed the bulb completely, rather than just hiding the filament. As Henningsen pointed out, this allowed the PH 5 to be used with any light source,[11] and indeed the lamp functions just as well with light sources that have been invented in more recent years, such as the energy-saving spiral fluorescent bulbs that were popular in the late twentieth century.

With few exceptions, such as the ceiling light for the 1959 *House of the Day After Tomorrow* exhibition,[12] Henningsen's lighting fixtures were designed for incandescent bulbs in their various forms. The same could be said of Arne Jacobsen and Verner Panton, although the latter lived until 1998, by which time lighting technology had developed significantly. A crucial invention was the halogen bulb (patented in 1959, but not popularized in Denmark until the 1980s)—a type of incandescent lamp that encloses a tungsten filament in a bulb of inert gas, mixed with a small amount of halogen. The halogen combines with the tungsten evaporated from the glowing filament to form a compound that is attracted back to the filament, so it doesn't condense on the bulb surface, and therefore the filament can last for longer.

Compared to the traditional incandescent bulb, the halogen bulb was also smaller, which opened up new possibilities for Louis Poulsen, notably with the 1987 Rappe Louis desk lamp by architect Alfred Homann (see page 201). But there were drawbacks too. The halogen bulb ran at a lower voltage than its predecessors, so it would last for longer, but at the same time required a transformer to be included within the lamp—in the case of the Rappe Louis, this was concealed within a thicker-than-usual base. It also produced a whiter light, which ran counter to the Danish preference for warmer, cosier illumination, and finally, it ran at higher temperatures, which came with additional design restrictions[13] (the problems with Henning Koppel's Bubi light, for example, would only have been exacerbated by a halogen source).

Opposite: A pair of drawings from the 1920s, comparing how light is reflected within a traditional trumpet screen lamp with a single conical shade, and the three-shade PH lamp.

Craft and Technology

Above: Henningsen in the Louis Poulsen showroom at Nyhavn 11 in
1939. Visitors were invited to put their faces against the metal ring
and read the text on the table, to experience the effect of the three-
shade lamp's diffuse light and soft shadows.

Opposite: A PH 3/2 table lamp among its constituent parts.

Craft and Technology

Opposite: A 1927 drawing by Danish poster artist Ib Andersen (1907-69), showing some important models in the PH system and their light distribution curves.

Above: The PH 3/2 Table lamp photographed at Salone del Mobile in Milan, Italy, 2019.

Craft and Technology

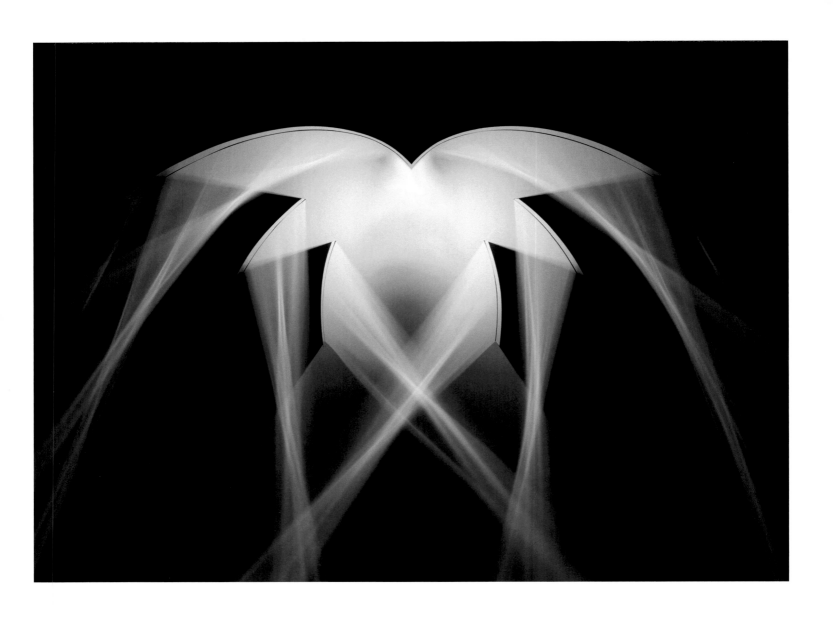

Above: A cross-section model of a three-shade PH lamp,
similar to the one Henningsen used in the 1964 short film *PH lys*
to demonstrate the three-shade system's merits.

Both the incandescent bulb and halogen bulb have since been phased out in favour of more energy-efficient and longer-lasting LEDs (light-emitting diodes)—the European Union began to phase out the incandescent bulb in 2009,[14] and the halogen bulb in 2018,[15] while the United States introduced legislation to similar effect in 2023.[16] Unlike incandescent and halogen bulbs, LEDs do not use a filament, but rather a semiconductor material that directly converts electricity into visible light without generating heat. In the almost three decades since 1996, when the first white LEDs were offered for sale,[17] the technology has matured to allow dimming and the changing of colour temperatures. LEDs can now take a wide range of forms, so there are variants that can fit lighting fixtures designed for older bulbs, as well as those that can be embedded so discreetly that they appear as pure beams of light.[18] This has liberated lighting companies and designers from previous constraints, and as we shall discuss in the next chapter, Louis Poulsen's contemporary designs, especially those by artist Olafur Eliasson and architect Anne Boysen, have taken ample advantage of LED technology (see pages 139 and 245). The low voltage requirement and thus low energy consumption of LEDs has further enabled Louis Poulsen to give new expressions to older designs, notably with the portable, battery-powered version of Verner Panton's Panthella (see page 172).

At the same time, technological advances have made certain design features within older Louis Poulsen lamps redundant: the red and blue internal shades of the PH 5, for instance, are no longer necessary, so it is a testament to the PH 5's other features that the lamp has remained in production and enjoyed continued fame. (Henningsen's 1962 Contrast lamp, which can provide a range of colour temperatures depending on the position of the same incandescent bulb, has not been so lucky, see page 91. It was dropped from the catalogue in 1991,[19] and given the ease of achieving warmer and cooler light within the same modern LED source, the lamp seems unlikely to make a comeback.)

Craft and Technology

Above and opposite: Henningsen's 1962 Contrast lamp, which can
provide a range of colour temperatures depending on the position
of the incandescent bulb—cooler, more blue light when the bulb is
raised and warmer, more red light when it is lowered. This is achieved
via the four different surface treatments on each of the ten shades:
white painted, blue, red and brightly polished.

MANUFACTURING TECHNOLOGIES

As light sources have evolved, so have manufacturing technologies used to create lighting fixtures, although here, the story is one of both continuity and change. The original PH lamp was available in copper (in various finishes) and soon after, opal glass—the former replacing the more expensive silver that Henningsen had used in the 1925 Paris lamp (see page 24). The stems and bases were usually made in cast iron or brass, and smaller elements such as socket holders and top covers were often in Bakelite, an early form of plastic.[20] In his later designs such as the 1942 Spiral lamp[21] and notably the PH 5,[22] Henningsen opted for aluminium—which is lighter and more pliable than copper—taking advantage of its increasing availability and decreasing production cost following the Second World War. Panton likewise favoured aluminium in his earlier designs such as the Topan and Moon pendants,[23] while Jacobsen's lighting, including the AJ series, was mostly in steel.[24]

Henningsen used glass for transparent and translucent surfaces, reserving acrylic for interior elements such as the red-striped tube within the 1949 Tivoli lamp.[25] In fact, Louis Poulsen made various prototypes of the PH 5 lamp with acrylic shades around 1958, but it never made it into production as the acrylic could not withstand the heat of the incandescent bulb. Meanwhile, two of Panton's most notable designs—the 1970 VP Globe (two clear acrylic hemispheres enclosing five curved aluminium shades, in a likely homage to Henningsen)[26] and the 1971 Panthella—both had acrylic shades.[27] This reflected advances in plastic manufacturing, but also Panton's knack for experimentation, which saw him create the world's first all-plastic chair in 1959.[28] Hans J. Wegner likewise created the shade of his 1973 Opala lamp in acrylic.[29] Affordable, lightweight and shatter-resistant, acrylic played an important role in expanding access to good lighting and thus, in the growth of the Louis Poulsen brand, through to the 2005 Collage pendant by designer Louise Campbell,[30] discussed in the next chapter. Acrylic's reputation has since suffered somewhat as the global mood has turned against plastic. Most plastics, including acrylic, can in fact be recycled, although our current recycling systems are not sophisticated enough and the quality of recycled plastics not high enough to warrant a renewed embrace of the material.

Opposite: Bottom bowls of Henningsen's 1958 PH 5 lamp at the Louis Poulsen factory in Vejen, Denmark.

Overleaf: The assembly room at the Louis Poulsen factory. The worker on the left is assembling a 2015 Patera lamp by Øivind Slaatto from strips of die-cut acrylic.

An extensive material palette has meant that Louis Poulsen has always relied on external suppliers to support its manufacturing: in the early years, the PH lamp utilized metal shades, frames and other metal components from the Lauritz Henriksen metal workshop in western Copenhagen (which had made the original Paris lamps), whereas the glass shades were made at De Forenede Glasværker (The United Glassworks) in Odense. As the lamp's popularity grew, more manufacturers were brought on board, including some in Germany, although the Second World War forced the company to revert to Danish production.[31] A purpose-built factory was inaugurated in Sluseholmen, in southern Copenhagen, in 1959, which would eventually grow to encompass the Lauritz Henriksen metal workshop, acquired by Louis Poulsen in 1942 following the retirement of the workshop's eponymous founder.[32] In 2005, compelled by the Copenhagen municipality to move out of its Sluseholmen factory in order to make way for a housing project, the company decided to move its manufacturing to a 16,000 sq m (4 acre) site in Vejen, south Denmark, previously occupied by the Austrian lighting group Zumtobel. The move stood in sharp contrast to a trend of outsourcing among Danish design brands—as the daily newspaper *Berlingske* reported then, it was a 'remarkable decision to maintain production in Denmark'.[33]

Around 85 per cent of Louis Poulsen's products continue to pass through the Vejen factory today, which employs around 135 blue-collar workers.[34] The factory focuses on metal production, and remarkably uses generations-old machinery and techniques alongside cutting-edge technology. For instance, a robotic arm—picking up flat sheets of aluminium, shaping them into trumpet-like forms and polishing the edges to form the top part of a PH 5 lamp—works alongside a craftsperson, operating a machine from 1941 and a basic set of tools to create similar forms.[35] The point in having old and new manufacturing processes in parallel is not only to sustain heritage methods, but also to ensure that the trickier elements can be produced to an adequate standard. For example, the shades of the 1979 Charlottenborg pendant—by architects Sophus Frandsen (1927–2013) and Ebbe Christensen (b. 1936), based on a four-shade design that Henningsen proposed in 1931[36]—have rolled edges and difficult angles that cannot be executed by robot to the same level of finesse as an experienced craftsperson.[37]

The custom machine dating back to 1970, used to sand and polish the leaves of the Artichoke lamp, likewise needs to be operated by a trained craftsperson. At a glance, its operational principle seems simple: two rolls of abrasive material (one a coarse sandpaper, the other one a finer Scotch-Brite) that run on a loop above an arched surface on which the Artichoke's leaves are placed. The craftsperson manipulates two metallic elements—one on top of each abrasive loop—by hand to achieve the desired finish on each leaf, whether it is made of copper, brass or stainless steel. While the process does not appear difficult to automate, there is a production advantage to doing this by hand, in that a trained craftsperson would be much more capable of noticing scratches, which can be quickly rectified before the leaves are sent to an adjacent area of the factory for assembly.

Opposite: PH 5 shades being prepared for painting at the Louis Poulsen factory.

Craft and Technology

Working by hand has a further advantage of allowing smaller production quantities where necessary—robots require meticulous programming to fulfil the desired tasks, which is not always effective for prototyping or for the creation of limited-edition products or colourways.[38]

But just as important is the intrinsic value of the human touch—while not all users may be concerned about whether a product is made by hand or entirely automated, the Louis Poulsen brand became successful in the 1920s for its humanistic design approach, which remains core to its ethos to this day. Embracing advanced manufacturing technologies while still employing highly skilled craftspeople, and indeed training new generations of them, distinguishes Louis Poulsen as a leading lighting company. It further affirms its reputation for products that are not only expertly designed, but also thoughtfully made.

Above: A close-up view of a twelve-drawer storage unit at the Louis Poulsen factory used to store the leaves of the PH Artichoke lamp. The number on each drawer indicates the layer (from top to bottom) that these leaves belong to, as the leaves of each layer are shaped differently.

Opposite: A copper PH Artichoke during assembly.

Into the Present

Above: Erik Magnussen's 1982 PorceLouis pendant, made by
Louis Poulsen in collaboration with porcelain factory Bing &
Grøndahl, stood apart from opal glass lamps in that its shade was
opaque white when switched off (left) and translucent when
illuminated (right).

THE LATE TWENTIETH CENTURY

Although the 1980s and 90s were a period of commercial success and international expansion for Louis Poulsen, it was not as significant a period for design compared to the mid-century. This was partly because of the brand's focus on professional lighting solutions rather than consumer-facing designs. It was also partly due to a sense of complacency that had emerged from being in possession of Poul Henningsen's and Verner Panton's catalogues, suggests Lisbeth Mansfeldt, Louis Poulsen's showroom manager and lighting expert from 1994 to 2018.[1] There are two key exceptions to the dearth of fresh designs: the 1982 PorceLouis by Erik Magnussen (1940–2014), and the 1987 Rappe Louis desk lamp by Alfred Homann (1948–2022).

Magnussen became a household name in Denmark in 1965 when he designed the Form 679 dinner service for Bing & Grøndahl, which became a bestseller for its stackable and heat-retaining properties.[2] Given his familiarity with porcelain's qualities, it makes sense that he would use the material for his collaboration with Louis Poulsen. The PorceLouis had a bell-shaped white shade with a flat top, which was slip-cast in one piece. Magnussen liked that the PorceLouis' humble design repeated well and would not dominate its space. Its simple form further allowed it to be made on existing machines at the Bing & Grøndahl porcelain factory that usually made mugs. Finally, the choice of material meant that the shade was an opaque white when the light was switched off, but would become translucent at night once it was illuminated—setting it apart from the many opal glass lamps on the market.[3]

Homann, an architect who studied under Vilhelm Wohlert (see page 155) and subsequently set up his own studio across Denmark and the United States, designed fifty different lighting fixtures across more than ten product lines, all for Louis Poulsen.[4] Most of these were outdoor lighting, but the Rappe Louis was conceived with domestic and office interiors in mind. The streamlined form of the lamp comprised a shade shaped like a duck's head, tapering into a slim, angled arm that bent into itself to form the base, all cast in plastic. The shade concealed a halogen pin bulb, a relative novelty that could produce a bright light despite its compact size, and an anodized aluminium reflector that focused the light downwards. Compared to that of a table lamp, the base was small, so the Rappe Louis could easily fit on to desks that were increasingly taken up by bulky computers.[5] While the lamp was innovative for its time, the rapid slimming down of electronic devices in the years since likely contributed to its discontinuation.

THE TWENTY FIRST CENTURY

Louis Poulsen's design story became more interesting from the early 2000s onwards, when the brand enlisted the design services of a new generation of creatives. Although varied and innovative in their approaches, they would stay true to the brand's time-honoured design philosophy, and occasionally pay homage to iconic products by the likes of Henningsen and Panton. They have taken advantage of advances in lighting technology, leveraged digital prototyping, embraced material innovation and at times blurred the boundaries between design and art, ushering Louis Poulsen into a new golden age.

LOUISE CAMPBELL

First among them is Danish-British designer Louise Campbell (b. 1970). 'When Louis Poulsen started collaborating with Louise, we were looking for new, younger designers who could uphold the legacy of our older designers and at the same time contribute their own, fresh ideas on light and design,' says Ulla Riemer, head of international training and education, who has worked at the brand since 1989.[6] Campbell fit the profile of their dream collaborator: she was energetic, eager to experiment, already had a measure of success with her seating designs (such as an upholstered indoor seesaw, intended to encourage social interaction in lounge and waiting areas) and, unlike most designers who had passed through Louis Poulsen's doors at that point, female. The latter was important not just as an attempt to rectify a long-standing demographic imbalance, but also because of the way Campbell imbues Scandinavian rationalism with a sense of femininity.

There was a slight problem: she had never designed lighting before and faced a rather steep learning curve. Riemer recalls many conversations with Campbell about the topics that had concerned Poul Henningsen in his time: the quality of light, how it can be manipulated and how to eliminate glare.[7] 'When Louis Poulsen called, I was young and unstoppably enthusiastic, while they were old and wise, which was a mutually beneficial combination,' Campbell recalls. 'They taught me, I challenged them. Louis Poulsen is very Danish, meaning local to me, allowing for a very close, hands-on collaboration. So I dedicated myself entirely to Louis Poulsen when it came to lighting design for many years.'[8]

Campbell's first design for Louis Poulsen was the 2004 Campbell pendant, which took design cues from Henningsen's PH Septima lamp (see page 106). Whereas PH Septima had seven glass shades, each with frosted and clear stripes radiating from the centre,[9] the Campbell pendant had just two similarly shaped shades of mouth-blown glass, one enclosing the other and held in place by magnets. Each of these had seven horizontal frosted stripes, which were layered so that the clear stripes of the outer shade overlay the frosted stripes of the inner shade, and vice versa.[10] As with the PH Septima, the use of frosted glass creates a diffuse light and prevents glare. A 2004 feature in *LP Nyt* introducing the Campbell pendant explained that the design is meant to capture 'some of the purest impressions we have when we experience outdoor light'. The designer further explained that the layering of shades created 'an interplay of the focal points [...] if we filter this light, we achieve the softness that distinguishes nature's light'. The Campbell pendant, 275 mm (11 inches) in diameter and 371 mm (14½ inches) high, was well suited for private homes as well as hospitality spaces.[11] It remained in production for eleven years.[12]

Opposite: Louise Campbell's 2005 Collage pendant, installed at a private residence in Aarhus, Denmark.

Into the Present

Opposite, left: A close-up of the laser-cut acrylic shades of Campbell's Collage pendant, evoking the way light in a forest passes through layers of foliage before it reaches the ground. Opposite, right: The Collage pendant in blue grey and dark green, installed at a private residence in Aarhus.

Above: The Collage pendant in hot lips at a private residence in Risskov, Denmark. The colour palette of the Collage pendant represented the shifting tastes in the public.

Above: The 2004 Campbell pendant was Danish-British designer
Louise Campbell's first lamp for Louis Poulsen, with seven horizontal
frosted stripes that pay homage to the seven glass shades of Poul
Henningsen's 1927–31 PH Septima lamp.

When Louis Poulsen unveiled the Campbell pendant for the first time that year, at the furniture fair at Copenhagen's Bella Center, it also showed a number of lighting studies by the designer. One of these was so popular that it was soon refined for production, becoming the 2005 Collage pendant and floor lamp. This pendant was likewise based on the filtering of light, specifically the way light in a forest passes through thousands of layers of foliage before it reaches the ground. Campbell devised a system of three staggered shades, cast in acrylic and laser-cut with a pattern of intersecting ellipses—some filled, others hollow. This ostensibly random pattern was in fact the result of repeated prototyping, both manually and on a computer. Campbell and Louis Poulsen's design team turned and repositioned the ellipses on each shade to get the layering right, so that there would be no direct view of the light source (and accordingly, no glare) from any angle. Together, the three layers created a depth of field, and a shadow play with a biophilic effect.

The cutting of the pattern posed another challenge. In a conversation with Campbell for *LP Nyt* that year, Louis Poulsen development engineer Rune W. Larsen explained that due to the limitations of mass-production technologies at the time, the shades had to be laser-cut as flat plates and then bent into shape. The size of the plates, the nature of the cut and the low tolerance limit made this a rather difficult process,[13] so the fact that Louis Poulsen persisted is testament to its drive for innovation. The colour palette of the Collage pendant pointed to shifting public tastes: while the Campbell pendant was only available in white, the Collage was launched in snow white, hot lips, heavenly blue, spring green, and smoke screen, with lemon yellow and juicy orange options added two years later.[14] In its embrace of pattern and colour, the Collage had more in common with the universe of Panton rather than that of Henningsen.

Besides the Collage, another Campbell light that remains in production at Louis Poulsen is the 2012 LC Shutters pendant. Here, the brief was to create an affordable and uncomplicated pendant that could be made at the brand's own factory in Vejen, which specializes in working with sheet metal (acrylic products are box build, meaning that individual parts are made elsewhere but assembled in Vejen). Despite its fine detailing, LC Shutters involves only three steps of production: an aluminium sheet is turned into the desired bell shape 'through several big fat custom-made machines', then the structure—with a lace-like trim at the top and bottom—and lattice pattern are simultaneously cut and pressed into form. The shade is finally spray-painted to achieve its white finish. These simple steps belie painstaking research and development over a two-year period. In a documentary video produced by Louis Poulsen around the launch of the lamp, Campbell explains its logic: 'by perforating the shade, we achieve a lamp that in itself glows as though lit up by many soft light sources. It is transformed from hard, solid, cold and dark, to light, soft and gentle.'[15]

Campbell also devised a more colourful version of the LC Shutters pendant, whereby acrylic inserts in various pastel hues would be applied on to some of the punched-in areas of the white aluminium shade.[16] This was not a spontaneous exercise, but rather followed a specific template from the designer. The LC Shutters Color, alongside the colourful versions of the Collage, have since been discontinued, leaving the white versions in the catalogue.[17]

Although Campbell has not released new lighting for Louis Poulsen in the decade since, product and design director Monique Faber credits her for having played a big role for the company, creating 'great designs that really hit at the perfect time'.[18] Likewise, the designer looks back fondly on her collaboration with Louis Poulsen, which involved weekly meetings for twelve years[19]: 'It is tough, the task of delivering design which is equally respectful and refreshing to a company which has such a loved, strong, classics-based history. And wonderful. [...] My confidence in practising the unusual art of allowing poetic angles to be found and highlighted within the form-follows-function rationality, which lies behind all good lighting design, grew over time. This knowledge, that intense long-term collaborations can lead to results which could never have been discovered if rushed, has stayed with me.'[20]

Above: Seen at a private residence in Stavanger, Norway, Campbell's 2012 LC Shutters pendant, with its perforated shade, is made from a single sheet of aluminium turned into a bell shape, cut and stamped at the Louis Poulsen factory in Vejen, Denmark.

CHRISTIAN FLINDT

Around the same time the Louis Poulsen design team approached Campbell as a new collaborator, it also found Christian Flindt (b. 1972), a recently graduated architect and designer who was exhibiting his final dissertation (a furniture project) at the 2003 Danish Furniture Fair. Again, Louis Poulsen took a gamble on an emerging talent and asked if Flindt could imagine himself designing lamps for the company. As Flindt recalls, it took a few years for him to 'get my head and hands readjusted to do lighting',[21] but the collaboration has paid handsome dividends. Flindt has since designed both indoor and outdoor lamps for Louis Poulsen, starting with a series of woven vinyl lamps.[22] His big success came in 2011 with the Flindt Bollard, a cast aluminium bollard with a long cut-out. The top of the cut-out conceals two LEDs that direct light downwards. The form of the cut-out not only reflects light outwards, but also creates a pleasing gradient—brighter at the top and dimmer at the bottom—that lends the bollard a sculptural quality. This was the first product in Louis Poulsen's outdoor collection to be made from scratch with LED technology. Initially commissioned for an exhibition in Viborg, in central Jutland, the bollard was put into wider production following positive feedback.[23]

As requests for a wall version flooded in, the designer would also develop the Flindt Wall, which appears to be cut out from a raised circle. Its cast metal construction makes it more resilient than most wall fixtures on the market, which are usually made of sheet metal or plastic. Again, the LED lights are concealed at the top of the cut-out, but this time a small slit at the top lets light out on to the wall behind it, creating an illuminated backdrop that makes the Flindt Wall appear to float. 'I thought of a sunset when I created the design,' Flindt recalls in a 2018 interview with *Reflections*, the successor to *LP Nyt*. 'When the sun is going down but is still too bright to look at, if you hold your hand out to cover it, you are suddenly able to see the gradient and colour of the sky beneath the sun. The Flindt Wall is, to me, a small sunset.' As a sign of evolving times, the development process involved not only computer modelling and metal casting, but also 3D printing to find the perfect balance between proportions, curves and light. The Flindt Wall is not only seen in outdoor locations across Denmark, including the Blue Planet Aquarium (Europe's largest aquarium, by local architects 3XN), it is suited to indoor spaces too.[24]

Opposite: The 2021 Flindt Garden Bollard, seen here in the colour Cor-Ten, is a variation of Danish designer Christian Flindt's 2011 Flindt Bollard, a cast aluminium bollard with a long cut-out that conceals the LED light source and directs light downwards.

Overleaf: The 2018 Flindt Wall installed along the entrance to the 3XN-designed Blue Planet Aquarium in Copenhagen, the largest aquarium in Europe.

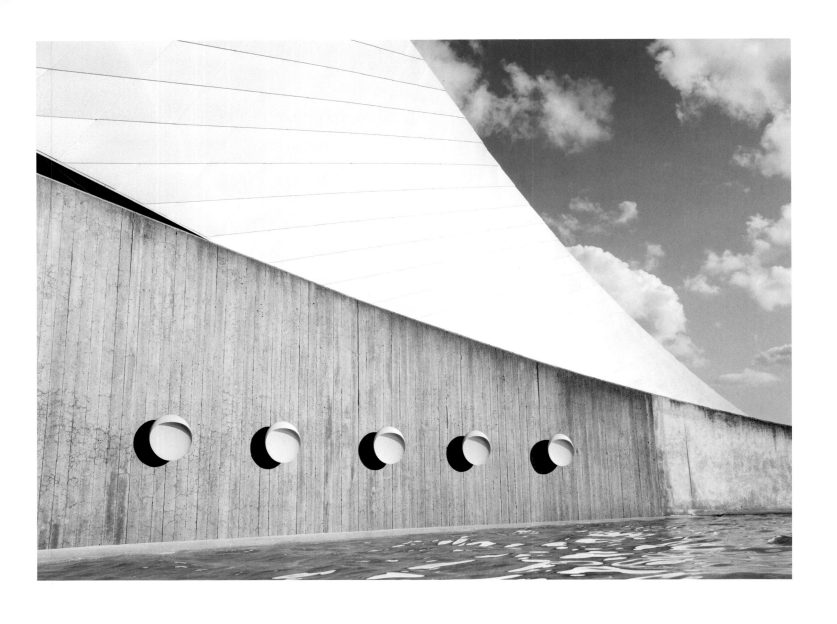

Into the Present

Above: A Louis Poulsen campaign image from 2018 shows the Flindt
Wall, released that year, being used inside.

Opposite: Flindt Wall outside the Blue Planet Aquarium, Copenhagen.

ØIVIND SLAATTO

While Campbell and Flindt joined Louis Poulsen's roster of designers at the brand's invitation, fellow Danish designer Øivind Slaatto (b. 1978) took the initiative to submit his portfolio to Louis Poulsen in 2008, a year after he graduated from the design school of the Royal Danish Academy of Fine Arts. He told Bettina Elbæk Pedersen, then design director of Louis Poulsen, that he had a new design for the brand, even though he didn't have one in hand. So, when Slaatto managed to get a meeting with Pedersen, he had to work around the clock for four days to come up with something—this would eventually become the Swirl lamp, which Louis Poulsen rejected but its competitor Le Klint gladly took up.[25] It is a decision that Louis Poulsen has likely come to regret: so iconic are the Swirl's spiral shades that the lamp appears next to the PH Artichoke lamp on the cover of *Danish Lights—1920 to Now* (see page 103). However, Pedersen was impressed with the way Slaatto worked and the effort that he had put into his student assignments and decided to work with him to develop a different design. This became the Patera, launched in 2015.

Slaatto calls the Patera 'a modern crystal chandelier'. 'I was curious to see if a chandelier could get another shape: one that would be timeless and even rounder than classic chandeliers, while at the same time having some of the magic of the traditional archetype,' he says of the lamp's origins.[26] The Patera has a globe-shaped structure like the sun, the original giver of light. This structure is hand-woven from die-cast acrylic, which has been shaped meticulously so its surface is built of small, diamond-shaped cells, laid out in a criss-cross spiral arrangement. The cells are positioned so that most of the light is pointed downwards—whereas a smooth globe would have distributed light evenly throughout its space. At the same time, the translucency of the acrylic gives the Patera a gentle 360-degree glow. There is no direct view of the light source, unless the viewer stands directly underneath the lamp.[27]

The Patera's distinctly contemporary appearance belies its reliance on the Fibonacci sequence, an arithmetic concept first used in the West by the medieval Italian mathematician Fibonacci to calculate the growth of rabbit populations. The concept is widespread in nature, from nautilus shells to spiral galaxies, but it took complex computer calculations to achieve the layout of the Patera's cells, which do not have any interior shadows—Slaatto has likened it to a three-dimensional Sudoku.[28] Of this process, the designer says, 'Louis Poulsen are very dedicated, interested in quality rather than in trends and fast results. Likewise, I want to do something that can last longer than I can imagine. I love to work until I'm done. Collaborating with a brand that appreciates this effort is wonderful.'[29]

While the Patera is often used on its own in private homes, some public and commercial spaces have used it in clusters, to evoke the sense of gazing up at a starry sky.[30] Slaatto has since developed further editions of the lamp, such as a limited-run silver version in 2019, inspired by his experience of designing lamps for the 2014 Eurovision Song Contest in Copenhagen,[31] and the Patera Oval in 2021, with an ellipsoid rather than spherical form that allows it to be installed in spaces with lower ceiling heights.[32]

Opposite: Danish designer Øivind Slaatto in his Copenhagen studio, with a 2015 Patera lamp for Louis Poulsen in the background.

Above: A row of Patera lamps installed at The Silo, a seventeen-storey grain silo in Nordhavn, Copenhagen, transformed into an apartment block by Cobe.

Opposite: A 2023 campaign image of the new edition of the Patera 300.

Into the Present

Opposite: The 2021 Patera Oval, whose ellipsoid form allows it to be installed in spaces with lower ceiling hights.

Above: The limited-edition Patera Silver lamp, released in 2019, owes its sparkling appearance to a silver-coloured reflective foil.

SHOICHI UCHIYAMA

While taking a chance on early-career designers within Denmark, and supporting their evolution into major talents, Louis Poulsen has also turned to international designers to broaden its roster—and in particular Japan, a country that shares the Danish affinity for good light and purchases more Louis Poulsen products than the almost-thrice-as-populous United States.[33] As Yoichi Nishio, editor-in-chief of the leading Japanese design and architecture magazine *Casa BRUTUS,* explains, Japanese audiences admire Denmark's history of design excellence, reverence of materials and craftsmanship, and commitment to sustainability, and therefore associate Danish design with an ideal lifestyle.[34]

In an early attempt at diversifying, Louis Poulsen enlisted the lighting designer Shoichi Uchiyama (b. 1947) to create the 2003 Enigma lamp, which deconstructs the chandelier concept into layers of disc-shaped concentric rings, with the largest forming the top layer and the smallest (a full disc, rather than a ring) at the bottom. At the top of the structure is a conical brushed aluminium fitting that conceals a downward light source.[35] The rays bounce back and forth the multiple discs, and in the process diffuse across the space to give an atmospheric light. The use of ultra-thin steel wire to hold together all the elements contributes to the lamp's hovering impression—'wings waft in the air', as the designer describes it.[36] The Enigma is a clear example of Japanese minimalism, while following Poul Henningsen's quintessentially Danish lighting principles.

Ulla Riemer, Louis Poulsen's head of international training and education, remembers that Uchiyama first submitted a drawing of the lamp in the early 2000s. 'He was describing how the light would be reflected from the shades, and what a beautiful atmosphere it would create, and it almost sounded too good to be true. Having made a model of the lamp according to Uchiyama's drawings, we realized that his description was actually correct.' The problem back then was that Louis Poulsen's strategy and budget were more directed at outdoor and office lighting, so it did not have the budget to work on the Enigma lamp. Fortunately, Uchiyama agreed that the brand could keep the design in its drawers and revisit it at a more suitable time.[37] The original four-shade pendant in 2003 was eventually followed by a seven-shade pendant for professional use, and a medium-sized five-shade pendant. Outsized versions of the seven-shade lamp, 5 m and 6 m (16½ and 20 feet) in diameter and with canvas shades to reduce weight, were even produced for a shopping centre in Granada, Spain, evidence of the Enigma's international appeal.

Opposite: An AW 2018 campaign photograph of Japanese designer Shoichi Uchiyama's seven-shade Enigma 825 pendant, intended for professional use.

NENDO

In the 2010s, Louis Poulsen would once again engage a Japanese design partner—this time nendo, the prolific studio that has worked across the creative spectrum, with clients including Issey Miyake, Cappellini and Lasvit. (Today, nendo's biggest claim to fame is probably the Olympic cauldron for the Tokyo 2020 Summer Olympics, a white orb that blossomed into a flower with ten reflective aluminium petals that amplified the flame's glow.)[38] For the 2015 NJP table lamp, nendo's chief designer Oki Sato (b. 1977) wanted to create a modern interpretation of Arne Jacobsen's AJ lamp (see page 126). The powder-coated aluminium shade of the NJP is shaped like a Santa's hat—a cone whose tip bends 90 degrees into a circular aperture, which serves a functional purpose: not only does the aperture release heat (so that users can comfortably swivel the shade), it also casts a soothing indirect light on the lamp's arm. In this, Sato paid homage to a characteristic feature of many Louis Poulsen lamps, which create both direct and atmospheric light. He also positioned the switch on the shade, under the aperture, rather than at the lamp's base, to encourage the user to adjust the light as they needed. In contrast to the shade, the arm is simple, with its thickness and rotation mechanisms carefully calibrated to enable smooth movement.[39] The NJP now comes in floor, wall and mini versions as well, and all iterations have a hidden timer function so the user can set the lamp to switch off after either four or eight hours. It adopts recent technologies, but not for technology's sake. As Sato explains, 'We didn't want to make something too technical using apps or sensors. We wanted something that people would understand as a lamp. It's very simple.'[40]

Opposite: The 2016 NJP floor lamp, by Japanese design studio nendo, features a powder-coated aluminium shade shaped like a Santa's hat. The lamp follows on from the NJP table lamp, launched the previous year.

Into the Present

Into the Present

Opposite and above: Louis Poulsen campaign photographs
from 2022 show new variations of nendo's NJP lamp: the NJP Mini
in petrol blue (above), and the NJP wall lamp in grey with a short
arm (opposite).

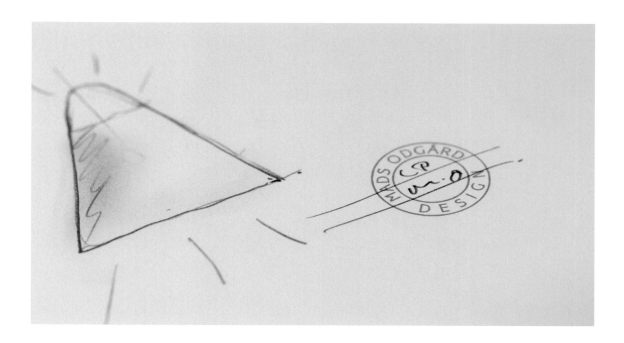

MADS ODGÅRD

Simplicity is likewise the motivating principle of the Above pendant, designed by Mads Odgård (b. 1960) in 2017. The Danish industrial designer has the distinction of having created Louis Poulsen's most widely produced product, which is not a lamp but rather a lamp canopy. Whereas traditional canopies are moulded in one piece, Odgård's 1994 'top hat' design comprises two identical half-cones that click together, inspired by a previous stint as a designer at Lego. The genius of Odgård's canopy is that it can come together or be removed at any step of installing or disassembling a light fixture. Over the years, Odgård has designed several indoor and outdoor lamps for Louis Poulsen, such as the 1999 Icon pendant, which hangs in thousands of locations in Denmark and abroad, but he is proudest of the Above pendant.

Above results from Odgård's ongoing obsession to create the most minimalist lamp possible that nonetheless carries Louis Poulsen's DNA. 'It's about functionality and personality, but also using less electricity and material. And when you eventually need to get rid of the lamp, you should only need to put it in one recycling bin,' he says. The resulting lamp has a single powder-coated aluminium shade, with a conical form and two cut-outs, which transform its rounded top into an arch and reveal its white interior. The arch gives a discreet ambient light, while the lamp's direct downward light can be tempered with an anti-glare shade, available separately. Odgård applauds Louis Poulsen for having taken a risk on such an overtly minimalist design: 'It takes courage for a company to produce and market the simplest thing.'[41]

Opposite: Danish designer Mads Odgård's minimalist 2017 Above lamp features a single conical shade with two cut-outs.

Above: A sketch of Odgård's Above lamp for Louis Poulsen.

CLARA VON ZWEIGBERGK

For Swedish designer Clara von Zweigbergk (b. 1970), inspiration came in the form of the onion-shaped domes on several of the buildings at Tivoli. Foremost among them was the 1909 restaurant and exhibition space by architect Knud Arne Petersen (1862–1943), who served as the amusement park's director. Drawing cues from Moorish palaces, Petersen had created a landmark with meticulously detailed arabesque walls, arched windows and an impressive central dome flanked by minarets, fronted by a garden with a circular fountain. Occupying a prime location just a stone's throw from Tivoli's main entrance, this is one of the first buildings that most visitors would encounter. Von Zweigbergk had in fact attended her first meeting with Louis Poulsen at Tivoli, and while she experimented with many ideas in the design process, she ultimately decided to draw from her initial impression. 'I made a lot of hand sketches, I made many paper prototypes. But in the end, I came back to this design that I had done, one of the first ones that I thought tied the story together,' she says of her abstracted Moorish dome, which she calls 'the Cirque'.[42]

While Tivoli's Moorish dome is illuminated by a lattice of light bulbs on its surface, Zweigbergk's pendant lamp uses a single light source to offer downward illumination. Each horizontal section, which has its own geometry, comes in a different colour, making this one of Louis Poulsen's more playful designs. A particularly eye-catching model has bands of red, light blue, teal and yellow. Such colour schemes are in fact a nod to the 'whirls and twirls' of Tivoli— 'carousels, candyfloss makers and wheels of fortune. When an object spins round very fast, the colours merge and end up being perceived as horizontal bands of colour,' the designer explains.[43] The circus-like effect is particularly evident when the lamps are installed in clusters, as they tend to be in larger spaces.

The ostensibly simple form of the Cirque was made possible by careful research: the aluminium shade is spun in one piece, which requires the use of a specially developed tool. And while the design may stand out among Louis Poulsen's typically more neutrally toned product range, a white lacquered inner reflector helps avoid glare and offers the technical finesse consumers have come to associate with the brand.

Previous page: The Icon Post by Mads Odgård, originally designed in 1999 for the small town of Flå in Norway, seen along Søllerødvej, Rudersdal, Denmark.

Opposite: Swedish designer Clara von Zweigbergk's 2016 Cirque pendant, inspired by the dome of architect Knud Arne Petersen's Moorish-style building for Tivoli Gardens.

GAMFRATESI

Like Odgård's Above pendant, the Yuh lamp was created in 2017. Designed by Danish-Italian design duo GamFratesi (Stine Gam, b. 1975, and Enrico Fratesi, b. 1978), it is similarly minimalist. Its painted aluminium shade is roughly conical, with a long opening at its top so that it could be raised and lowered, inclined and declined, and rotated along the lamp's upright stem. The base is circular, to harmonize with the conical shade, and a visible cord connects the top of the shade to the lower part of the stem, curving at a pleasing angle as the lamp is lowered. Gam explains that the design was inspired by Arne Jacobsen: 'We took the horizontal line from the shade on the AJ lamp, and once that was drawn, everything else almost fell into place.'[44] As with the NJP and Above lamps, the top opening also served to create an ambient light that brought the design in line with Henningsen's lighting principles.

The movement of the shade, which gave the lamp its name ('Yuh' is a phonetic form of the English 'you', inviting the user to manipulate the lamp as they wished),[45] proved a test of Louis Poulsen's expertise and willingness to innovate. As Fratesi recalls, 'We almost drove the engineers at Louis Poulsen crazy. Six of them were assigned to the task. The engineers then came back to us with lots of technical parts, which we then assessed, and that's how it proceeded until we arrived at the final product.'[46]

While the Yuh was initially commissioned as a table and floor lamp, GamFratesi realized that it would also work as a wall lamp. The initial versions were in black and white.[47] In 2019, they released new versions with brass stems, and bases in Nero Marquina marble to match the black shade, and Carrara marble to match the white one. These material changes made the Yuh lamp suitable for a wider range of spaces, in keeping with GamFratesi's intentions to make as flexible a lamp as possible.

Opposite, above: Danish-Italian design duo GamFratesi in their Copenhagen studio with drawings of their 2017 Yuh lamp.

Opposite, below: Variations of GamFratesi's Yuh lamp released in 2019, with brass stems and bases in black Nero Marquina marble and white Carrara marble.

Opposite: A 2019 campaign image showing GamFratesi's Yuh lamps, in floor version in monochrome white and table version in monochrome black.

Above: A close-up view of GamFratesi's Yuh lamp in monochrome black.

OLAFUR ELIASSON

Given Poul Henningsen's multitude of talents and interests, it is not surprising that art has long been part of Louis Poulsen's DNA. Already in 1943, two years after *LP Nyt* was founded, Henningsen would use a colour screen print based on the painting *Arrangement* by Vilhelm Lundstrøm (1893–1950), which he owned, to illustrate how colours would vary under different lighting conditions: daylight, incandescent light, quartz light and nitrate light.[48] Meanwhile, the fiftieth anniversary issue of the company magazine featured a special cover by another preeminent Danish painter, Per Kirkeby (1938–2018). It was printed as an eight-colour lithograph and individually numbered, making it a collector's item.[49] The brand further stepped up its engagement with the arts in 2019, when it teamed up with Olafur Eliasson (b. 1967) on the OE Quasi—the brand's first product created by a world-renowned artist, and Eliasson's first lighting fixture for a major manufacturer.[50]

It was a match made in heaven. Not only is the Icelandic-Danish Eliasson one of the best artists of this century (the legendary art critic Peter Schjeldahl wrote in 2008 that Eliasson was 'so much better than anyone else in today's ranks of

Opposite: Icelandic-Danish artist Olafur Eliasson with his 2019 OE Quasi lamp for Louis Poulsen, his first lighting design for a major manufacturer, at Copenhagen fishmonger Kødbyens Fiskeslagter.

Above: A detail of the OE Quasi lamp in the Terrace Bar at Tate Modern, London.

crowd-pleasing installational artists that there should be a nice, clean, special word other than "art" for what he does, to set him apart'[51]), he made his name as an expert manipulator of light, famously installing an artificial sun within the Turbine Hall at London's Tate Modern, made of more than two hundred light bulbs, facilitated by mirrors and a mist machine.[52] *The weather project*, as that 2003 work was titled, was a major cultural moment that also articulated a new vision of museums as public spaces. Adding to Eliasson's qualifications was his well-established interest in architecture and design, which brought him closer to Louis Poulsen's existing roster. He ran an architecture studio, Studio Other Spaces, which has worked on projects from Ilulissat, Greenland to Addis Ababa, Ethiopia,[53] and already had form with lighting design projects, such as *Opera house chandeliers*, 2004, for Copenhagen Opera House.[54] As a bonus, there was a social dimension to his work that aligned with the legacy of Poul Henningsen—such as hauling Greenlandic ice blocks to major European cities to drive home the devastating reality of climate change,[55] and creating portable solar-cell lamps for communities without electricity in Sub-Saharan Africa.[56]

Eliasson's OE Quasi not only drew on his study of light, it also expanded on his experiments with geometric patterns, such as his *Facade for Harpa Reykjavik Concert Hall and Conference Centre*, 2013, reminiscent of the crystalline basalt columns often found in Iceland. Its outer frame, made of aluminium, is an icosahedron—with twenty triangular faces and twelve vertices. Appearing to float inside is a white polycarbonate reflector, shaped like a dodecahedron—with twelve pentagonal faces and twenty vertices. Rather than suspending a light source at the centre of the reflector, Eliasson elected to embed them in the inner vertices of the aluminium frame, and connect them with light guides along the inner edges. The light is thus directed towards the reflector, creating uniform illumination in all directions. He explained the design as follows in a interview in *Wallpaper**: 'Normally you would have a structure on the inside surrounded by a soft skin cladding the light, but my ambition was to reverse this, so you first see the outer structure holding the lamp together, with the soft reflecting material on the inside. Presenting the structure in this way also feels more honest, more revealing. It looks quite magical, but really there is no magic, no tricks, no secrets.'[57]

The reversed structure is 'different from what Poul Henningsen would have done,' says Monique Faber, Louis Poulsen's director of product and design. 'It was a nice way to pay homage to Henningsen, but also turn it around in a way.'[58] For the CEO Søren Mygind Eskildsen, the collaboration with Eliasson was a way to renew Louis Poulsen's heritage: 'Besides relaunching existing products, we strive to bring something new to the brand, and see what can be done with the right collaborator, who can play in our design philosophy. To see Olafur create an artwork while maintaining an excellent quality of light has been inspiring.'[59]

Beyond its experimentation with form and function, the OE Quasi is also notable for its sustainable qualities: the aluminium used is 90 per cent recycled, and the design allows for future disassembly, so individual elements can be replaced as necessary to extend the product's life, and with residual parts sent for recycling. 'I wanted to create a product that doesn't produce any waste and that people will keep forever,' Eliasson explained.[60]

Above: Eliasson created three identical chandeliers in 2004 for the foyer of Henning Larsen Architects' Copenhagen Opera House, each comprising 1,430 pieces of colour-effect filter glass.

Although the OE Quasi has an impressive diameter of 896 mm (35 inches), making it slightly bigger than the original PH Artichoke lamp, Faber explains that the goal was never to make a blockbuster; rather, it was to align Eliasson's approach with Louis Poulsen's.[61] In its elegant shaping of light, as well as its balancing of mathematical rigour and sculptural beauty, the OE Quasi fulfils this task magnificently. And while its size may prevent it from being installed in most homes, the lamp found the perfect showcase the same year at the Tate Modern's Terrace Bar. Four examples were suspended above a long communal dining table, to coincide with Studio Olafur Eliasson Kitchen's takeover of the space and the artist's solo exhibition in the galleries upstairs.[62] It was an eloquent demonstration of how good light—like good art and good food—can bring people together.

Above: Eliasson's geometric *Facade for Harpa Reykjavik Concert Hall and Conference Centre*, 2013, is based on a modular, space-filling structure called the quasi brick, and incorporates colour-effect filter glass.

Opposite: Eliasson's 2003 work, *The weather project,* in the Turbine Hall at London's Tate Modern, used more than two hundred light bulbs to create an artificial sun.

ANNE BOYSEN

Louis Poulsen's newest product shares some of the OE Quasi's artistic qualities, but comes from a more emerging creative talent and has an entirely different backstory. In 2020, the Danish architect Anne Boysen (b. 1980) entered *Denmark's Next Classic*, a televised competition organized by DR1, the flagship television channel of the Danish Broadcasting Corporation, to identify new furniture and lighting that can hold a candle to the country's mid-century icons. One of the competition briefs, to create a floor lamp that could shape a space, led her to create the Moonsetter lamp, which then made her the programme's winner. Boysen subsequently brought the Moonsetter to Louis Poulsen, as she considers it the best lighting manufacturer in the Nordics and admires its attention to detail. The brand then worked with her on the final design iterations and in 2021 launched the lamp in a limited edition of one hundred.[63]

Geometrically, the Moonsetter is much more rudimentary than the OE Quasi: comprising a cylindrical base, laid on its side, intersecting the corner of an upright square frame—both made from chrome-plated aluminium. A circular disc (chrome-plated on one side, white on the other) appears to have been cut out from the centre of the square, held in place by a single axis that allows it to rotate 360 degrees. A LED light source is submerged across half the interior arc. The joy of the Moonsetter is that the user can play around with the disc to adjust how light is disseminated: it varies when reflected on the chrome-plated surface and when diffused on the white one, and depending on the angle of displacement from the frame.[64] Parallels can be seen with Verner Panton's Moon pendant, whose ten aluminium rings could be adjusted as the user desired (see page 166), but the Moonsetter goes further, in that the user can also brighten or dim the light through a rotatable switch on the cylindrical base—best operated by foot—making the Moonsetter a tactile design that engages the whole body.[65] It's a functional piece of lighting, as well as a kinetic artwork that invites continuous exploration and learning.

Boysen explains the Moonsetter's origins as such: 'I was at my desk one night when I suddenly saw it. A ray of moonlight shone through a gap in the curtains. I put different surfaces in front of it and became fascinated with how something white produced a diffused reflection of light, and mirror, quite another type of reflection. So I asked myself, how do you simplify this into an accessible idiom, making the complex simple and intuitive?'[66]

Louis Poulsen's Monique Faber admits that the decision to take on the Moonsetter was a bold step for the brand. It's not a typical lamp, and its approach to lighting differs sharply from Henningsen's. 'Of course, it's not a typical reading light, or one that can symmetrically distribute light in a space. What I love is that it gives you both directed light and reflected light, which you can manipulate as you wish. It's asking questions, and inspiring conversations: what is light? Why do we want it, why do we need it, and how do we use it?'[67]

Opposite: Danish architect and designer Anne Boysen with her Moonsetter lamp, created in 2020 for *Denmark's Next Classic*, a televised competition organized by the Danish Broadcasting Corporation.

Like the OE Quasi before it, the Moonsetter takes the Louis Poulsen brand in a new direction. Certainly, this artistic turn requires a faith in innovation, and a level of investment that Louis Poulsen's more conservative peers would have been reluctant to commit. The limited-edition size also suggests that the brand is not expecting handsome financial gain on this occasion. But the Moonsetter's aesthetic merits, its playful qualities and its ability to enhance our appreciation of light certainly encourage us to look at Louis Poulsen with fresh eyes, which is a reward of a different sort. It reminds us that the Louis Poulsen of today continues to be as forward-thinking as it was in Henningsen's time. That the OE Quasi and Moonsetter are the only two brand-new products Louis Poulsen has launched within a four-year period, within an industry that operates on annual cycles, is not a bad thing either. After all, Louis Poulsen can draw on an impressive catalogue of older designs, which allow it to tap into a wider audience than ever before as the international embrace of Nordic design continues. Whether by relaunching long-discontinued pieces from its archive (such as Henningsen's PH Septima, brought back in 2020 following an eight-decade hiatus),[68] by making incremental improvements that enhance the functionality of existing products, or by introducing new sizes and colourways to accommodate evolving demands, the brand already has a solid business based on its rich heritage. This offers Louis Poulsen the freedom to experiment with new designs as it sees fit, but also the freedom to only put such designs into production where it deems them of exceptional quality.

Such a strategy doesn't only benefit customers, who can be assured of the merits of new Louis Poulsen releases. It also benefits design collaborators, who have been invariably enthusiastic in their evaluation of the brand. As Boysen says, 'Louis Poulsen has taught me never to compromise on design or light quality. If you want to create a classic, it's about getting all parameters to come together in a higher unity. The world does not need more lamps, but better light and better design.'[69]

Christian Flindt concurs: 'If you catch Louis Poulsen on a good day, they are a company that is willing to go all the way to realize and refine your project—in a way that only a few other companies in the world will or can do. As a designer this is the best.'[70]

Opposite: A Louis Poulsen campaign photograph from 2022 showing Boysen's Moonsetter lamp, which entered the brand's catalogue the previous year.

Home and Beyond

Home and Beyond

EARLY CATALOGUES

While Louis Poulsen's products over the past century could have stood on their own merits, their popularity and stature, both in Denmark and abroad, owe much to judicious marketing. When the first PH lamps arrived in 1926, the catalogue was published in four languages—Danish, English, French and German, evidence of Sophus Kaastrup-Olsen's ambitions for the Louis Poulsen business. Its title, *Modern Lighting*, and the cover image, which showed the PH lamp in cross-section with lines indicating how light emanating within the bulb would be reflected by the shades, corresponded to Henningsen's form-follows-function approach.[1]

Within the decade, the brand would publish further catalogues for the Belgian, Argentinian, Spanish, Hungarian, Dutch and Czech markets, making it one of the first Danish manufacturers to achieve such a global reach. Comparing the covers of such local catalogues, we can already see a range of marketing approaches. Continuing the approach of the original catalogue, a 1928 German catalogue overlays a line drawing with the giant letters 'PH' printed in yellow, and the cover lines 'Lichtquelle // Leuchte // Beleuchtung' ('Light source // light // illumination'), with additional text emphasizing how changes in each of these areas are calling for a new lighting system. A British catalogue from the same year takes a more straightforward approach to promoting the PH system, accompanying its illustration of a lamp with the title 'Scientific Interior Lighting' and the subheading 'for offices, churches, halls, shops, factories, assembly rooms & domestic use'. Meanwhile, a 1929 Belgian catalogue, which shows the lamp from two different angles, highlights its aesthetic merits: *La Beauté par la ligne strictement constructive de la lampe* ('Beauty through the strictly constructed lines of the lamp'), it read. More confident is a Dutch catalogue from the late 1920s, whose typographic cover, elaborate enough to not be a cost-saving measure, suggests the broad name recognition that the PH lamps already enjoyed at the time.[2]

Opposite: Poul Henningsen's 1926 Forum lamp, as featured on the cover illustration of a Louis Poulsen catalogue in the same year. The catalogue title reads 'Modern Light // PH System'.

Erfreulich...

LICHTQUELLE
LEUCHTE
BELEUCHTUNG

Opposite: A 1939 Louis Poulsen catalogue for the German market, with the slogan 'Erfreulich…' ('Pleasurable').

Above: A 1928 catalogue, also for the German market, with the cover lines 'Lichtquelle // Leuchte // Beleuchtung' ('Light source // light // illumination') and additional text emphasizing how changes in each of these areas call for a new lighting system.

Above, clockwise from top left: A British catalogue for the three-shade PH lamps from 1927, featuring a light diffusion diagram; a Dutch catalogue from 1929; and a Spanish catalogue from the late 1920s with the cover line 'What is a PH lamp?'.

Opposite: A collage of various Louis Poulsen advertisements for the PH system.

Home and Beyond

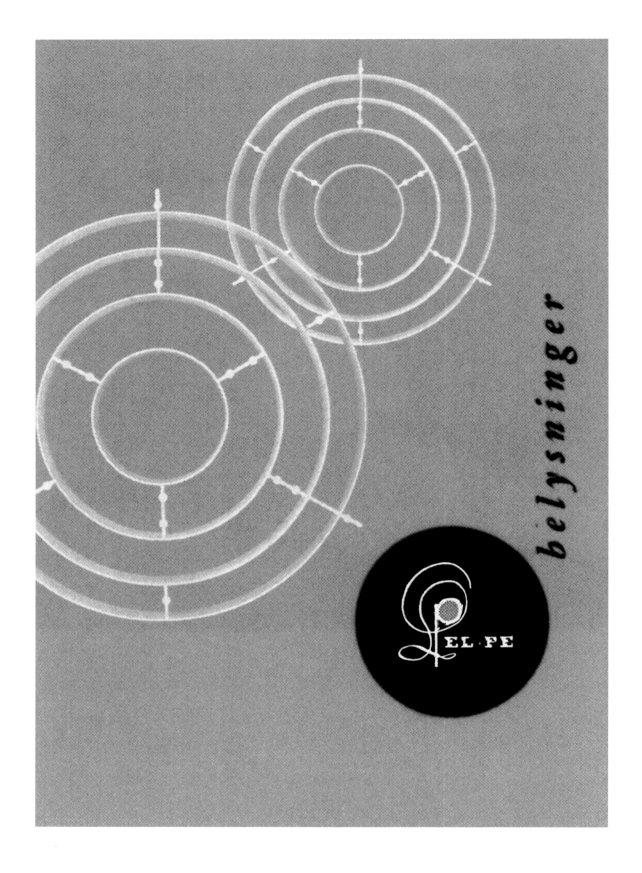

belysninger

EL·FE

EL·PE LYSRØRSARMATURER

Opposite: The cover of a Louis Poulsen catalogue from 1954, featuring drawings of a four-shade lamp by Henningsen viewed from below, and the 1942 logo by Johan Pedersen.

Above: Another catalogue from the same year dedicated to fluorescent fixtures.

NYT 1941-1991

OTTE SMAA SIDER, LP NYT AND REFLECTIONS

More important than Louis Poulsen's catalogues are the brand's publications over the years, which have been creative and often educational platforms to heighten brand awareness and reinforce customer loyalty. Before *LP Nyt*, there was *Otte Smaa Sider* (*Eight Small Pages*), a small publication that existed between 1926 and 1929. Its stated goal was 'to improve taste, entice our customers away from the more insipid American style of advertising, which sees the advertisement's sole task as being to hammer home a name [...] while failing miserably to offer a matter-of-fact description of how good the over-advertised object happens to be'. Although the publication was text-heavy and at times onerous, it had its humorous moments: a 1926 feature on bacon production emphasized the need for Danish pigs to be fed warm breakfasts, which turned out to be a way to promote an electric pig feed heater sold by Louis Poulsen, which could warm up the feed overnight when electricity rates were lower.[3]

In comparison, *LP Nyt*—particularly under Henningsen's editorship from 1941 until his death in 1967—had a much broader remit, not only as an advertising forum but also as a platform for critical and informative features. There were the expected features on light bulbs and electrical plugs, buildings that had recently introduced Louis Poulsen products, and life at the Louis Poulsen headquarters at Nyhavn 11. However, this was supplemented by more idiosyncratic content, on the paintings of Vilhelm Lundstrøm and the (non-Louis Poulsen) lighting in old churches, for instance, which served to emphasize the importance of good lighting; regular letter exchanges between Henningsen and his contemporaries; and reader feedback, both positive and negative, edited according to the motto 'disagreement makes us strong'.[4]

Leafing through the magazine's archives, we can not only get a sense of how Louis Poulsen's lighting has evolved, but also see the arrival of modernity through first-hand reports of the opening of landmarks such as the Langelinie Pavilion, SAS Royal Hotel and more. As art journalist Lisbeth Bonde observed in an essay surveying *LP Nyt*'s first sixty years, 'the magazine was full of new, cultural amenities, i.e. the right, tight settings and lines based on the right culturally radical ideas and discussed over gourmet cuisine in the company of good friends and with a real fire crackling in the brick fireplace.'[5]

Post-Henningsen, Louis Poulsen continued to invest handsomely in *LP Nyt*, which continued its exploration of how space and lighting inform human wellbeing. Colour photography arrived in 1972, in time for vivid reports of Verner Panton's show-stopping interior projects; at the same time, the art direction also evolved to put a greater emphasis on visuals, with full-bleed, image-led covers that affirmed Louis Poulsen's commitment to quality, emphasized *LP Nyt*'s categorization as a magazine rather than a newsletter, and put it on a strong footing vis-à-vis international design titles (it helped that subscriptions to *LP Nyt* remained free, as they had been from the start).

Opposite: The invitation to the fiftieth anniversary celebrations of *LP Nyt* in 1991, which included an exhibition by journalist Paul Hammerich (1927-92), who had written a biography of Henningsen five years before.

As Louis Poulsen expanded its footprint abroad, so the content of *LP Nyt* diverged from the bread and butter of Danish construction and design. The subjects of later architecture features ranged from the Ministry of Foreign Affairs in Riyadh, designed by Henning Larsen; the American Center in Paris, by Canadian-American architect Frank Gehry (b. 1929; the building is now home to the Cinémathèque Française); a 300-year-old ryokan in Kyoto that is often considered Japan's finest; even a 4,000 sq m (43,000 sq foot) hotel in northernmost Lapland, built entirely from ice and snow. Varied though these buildings were, they had one thing in common: the use of Louis Poulsen products, which accentuated the building features and made the user experience all the more pleasurable. The aim, naturally, was to show how successful the company had become, but at the same time enlightening, entertaining and inspiring an ever-growing audience.

And grow it did: an English edition of *LP Nyt* was launched in 1996, soon followed by German and Japanese versions.[6] This expansion was accompanied by a broadening of its contributor pool, which was no longer limited to the finest design and architecture writers and practitioners within Denmark: a 1998 feature on the role of light in Japanese architecture, for instance, was penned by Tokyo-based architect Noriyuki Asakura.[7]

An evolving media landscape meant that into the mid-2000s, *LP Nyt* decreased in frequency, with its final issue published in 2012. A new magazine launched in 2017, titled *Reflections*, has a tighter focus on the brand and its products, forgoing the longer-form features that characterized *LP Nyt* in favour of sumptuous photo shoots that show Louis Poulsen lighting in a wide range of settings. Keeping in step with the times, *Reflections* has also launched a video channel, featuring documentary-style videos that showcase contemporary creatives discussing classic designs such the Panthella lamp, and recent collaborators such as Christian Flindt and SAGA Space Architects offering first-hand insights into their projects.[8]

Opposite, clockwise from top left: Covers of *LP Nyt*, featuring a caricature of Henningsen on what would have been his nintieth birthday (1984); Alfred Homann's Rappe Louis table lamp (1987); an eight-colour lithograph by Danish painter Per Kirkeby (1991, for the fiftieth anniversary issue); and the AJ Table lamp at Herzog & de Meuron's IKMZ University Library in Cottbus, Germany (2006).

PH i nyt lys

Den 9. september ville Poul Henningsen være fyldt 90 år. Om sådan noget skal markeres eller ej er en smagssag - og NYT bruger det udelukkende som en kærkommen anledning til at sætte focus på den, der mere end nogen anden har betydet noget for belysningens udvikling her i Danmark.

PHs samtidige fortæller om dengang, det hele begyndte - og repræsentanter for firser-generationen sætter nyt lys på: det radikale standpunkts tusindkunstner og gudfather, arkitekten, samfundsrevseren, kulturredpiskeren og den gamle demokrat, der trækker den røde tråd mellem Georg Brandes og Kulørte Klat: her destilleret i et sindsbillede af tegneren Anne Marie Steen-Petersen.

405

Nyhavn 11, 6. august 1984

588

THE LOUIS POULSEN MAGAZINE OF LIGHTING AND ARCHITECTURE 2006 583

The University Library, IKMZ, in Cottbus

Light and architecture in Edinburgh

FDA at Irvine

louis poulsen

1941-1991

Nr. 13468

Home and Beyond

EXHIBITIONS

Since the 1925 International Exhibition of Modern Decorative and Industrial Arts in Paris (see page 24), exhibitions have played a critical role in the dissemination of Louis Poulsen's designs. The fact that many such exhibitions have been geared primarily towards trade audiences has not deterred the brand from going above and beyond in both content and exhibition design.

A dive into the brand's archives reveals impressive plans and photographs from such exhibitions: at an exhibition in Cologne, Germany in 1928, forty-eight PH lamps were installed in a giant spiral helix around a tall column. So successful was this installation that PH lamps were installed throughout Cologne's Central Station the following year.[9] Meanwhile, at the Ideal Homes exhibition at Copenhagen's Forum in 1934, display cases were dwarfed by 10 m (30 foot) tall letters spelling out 'PH', better to project Henningsen's dominant position among a generation of designers.[10] Later designers carried on this tradition: Verner Panton stole the show at the furniture fair at Copenhagen's Bella Center in 1972, presenting his futuristic lighting models such as the Panthella, Flowerpot and VP Globe lamps alongside his new Pantonova wire furniture, in a joint stand for Louis Poulsen and Fritz Hansen.[11] The stand was notable for its presentation of interior environments rather than individual pieces, and in signature Panton style, was dressed in vivid shades of red and blue. Moving into the recent past, Louis Poulsen commissioned GamFratesi for its stand at 2017's Euroluce, the lighting design exhibition in Milan, Italy, held biannually alongside the Salone del Mobile design fair. The duo created a double-height architectural structure, simultaneously evoking Japanese origami and Indian step wells, to encourage visitors to ponder how cuts, lines and shapes inform light and ambience. It was a show-stopping setting in which to display the new Yuh lamps (see page 235) alongside iconic mid-century designs from the brand's catalogue.[12]

More significant, of course, are exhibitions meant for the general public. After the Paris Exhibition, there was the 1929 International Exposition in Barcelona, Spain, which is best remembered for its German Pavilion designed by Ludvig Mies van der Rohe and Lilly Reich (1885–1947)—it is simply referred to as the Barcelona Pavilion today. At this expo, Louis Poulsen had its own stand within the Danish Pavilion, where it showcased the full PH range with all shade sizes and lamp types. A traditional pleated lamp shade was deliberately included to accentuate the modern nature of Henningsen's designs.[13] It was on this occasion that the PH lamps won the prestigious Grand Prix. Three decades later, it would be the PH Artichoke lamp that took centre stage at the Danish Pavilion at the 1960 Triennale di Milano.[14]

Opposite: A drawing from August 1928 showing forty-eight PH lamps installed in a giant spiral helix around a tall column, realized at an exhibition in Cologne, Germany, later that year.

Opposite: Verner Panton created a joint stand for Louis Poulsen and furniture manufacturer Fritz Hansen for the furniture fair at Copenhagen's Bella Center in 1972, presenting his recent designs for Louis Poulsen, including the Panthella, VP Globe and Spion lamps, alongside his new Pantonova wire furniture for Fritz Hansen. ©Verner Panton Design AG.

Above: Panton at the joint stand at the Bella Center, sat underneath his Spion and Topan lamps for Louis Poulsen. ©Verner Panton Design AG.

Opposite: At the Ideal Homes exhibition at Copenhagen's Forum in 1934, 10 m (30 foot) tall letters spell out 'PH'.

Above: The PH Artichoke taking centre stage at the Danish Pavilion at the 1960 Triennale di Milano, alongside a PK31 sofa by Poul Kjærholm.

Home and Beyond

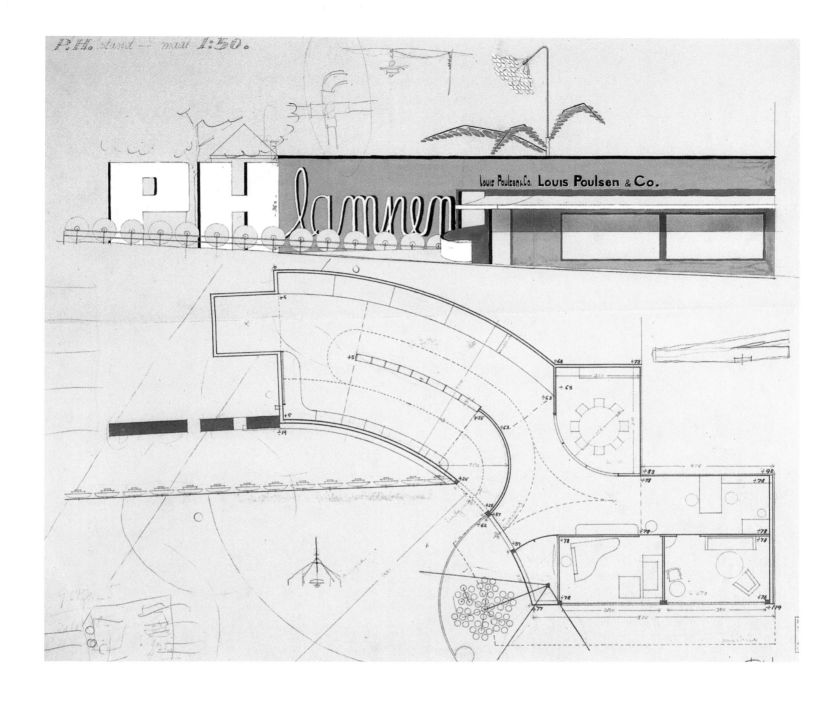

Opposite: The entrance to an exhibition of PH lamps at Tivoli Gardens, photographed in 1931. The letters 'PH lampen' (PH lamps) are illuminated by a row of tilted three-shade lamps.

Above: German architect Hans Hansen's (1889-1966) plans for the same exhibition, featuring a building that curved in the same way as Henningsen's lamp shades. The flower-shaped installation perched atop the building featured green 'leaves' formed from PH lamps of various sizes.

Above: A house created by Henningsen, architect Ole Helweg
and Swedish designer Torsten Johansson (1917-96) for *The House of
the Day after Tomorrow*, a 1959 exhibition at Copenhagen's Forum.
The installation featured a custom-made ceiling light by Henningsen
and Louis Poulsen, with overlapping aluminium shades painted
white, yellow and red, and a fluorescent light source.

Such presentations not only confer prestige to the brand, they also affirm its position among the avant-garde. Just as Arne Jacobsen's AJ Reading lamp was created in 1929 for (and emerged victorious in) the House of the Future competition organized by the Danish Architects' Association (see page 121),[15] three decades later, Henningsen collaborated with Louis Poulsen on a fluorescent pendant for the *House of the Day after Tomorrow* exhibition, also at Copenhagen's Forum. On this occasion, architect Ole Helweg (1916–2001) created a dome-shaped house to represent his vision for an interior of the future and enlisted Henningsen to work on the lighting. Henningsen, who had been vocal in his opposition to fluorescent lighting, took the opportunity to explore whether fluorescent light sources could be manipulated to create good light. The resulting lighting stands apart from every other Henningsen lamp in its design: although based on the Artichoke (designed the year before), this one had seven overlapping rather than staggered layers of leaves, coming together to create an asymmetrical form. Their configuration may appear haphazard, but was in fact carefully devised to distribute light evenly. The key feature of this lamp, however, was the colouring of the shades: white at the top, yellow in the centre and red at the base. Fluorescent lighting tends to interfere with colour perception, so once the light source is switched on, the shades appear to be blue, green and red instead—not coincidentally the three primary colours of light. This 'unrealistic poem of the fluorescent tube's possibilities', as Henningsen calls it, was only released in an edition of twenty, and remains highly sought after today (see page 57).[16]

Given the brand's deep association with Japan, it is not surprising that one of its most significant public exhibitions took place at the Mori Art Museum in Tokyo in November 2004, coinciding with a state visit by Queen Margrethe II of Denmark. *Styling Danish Life*, as the exhibition was titled, was a collaboration with three other Danish heritage brands: Fritz Hansen, Royal Copenhagen and Bang & Olufsen. The task of designing this exhibition went to Tadao Ando (b. 1941)—by then already a Pritzker Architecture Prize winner, making the commission a veritable coup for the four brands. Ando was given free rein to configure the 27 × 9 m (90 × 30 foot) exhibition space and select all the design products displayed within it. He created a wall unit and a series of cubic galleries, all in white and blue, and among the products he chose were Louis Poulsen's PH Artichoke, Snowball and PH 5 lamps, all by Henningsen; Enigma, by Shoichi Uchiyama; and (the since discontinued) Charisma, by PLH Design. The Japanese architect expressed a love and kinship with these products, which affirmed the Danish belief that the key to a good life is to surround oneself with objects of functional beauty. 'The architectural and furniture design from Scandinavia has always been very close to me,' Ando said in an interview with *LP Nyt*. He further praised Henningsen's lighting designs: 'I can feel their original cultural climate, the respect for tradition and the will for the future, and the thoughts of the designer who struggled with various themes in developing the fixtures. [...] To make daily life affluent by caring for light, that's a wonderful thing.'[17]

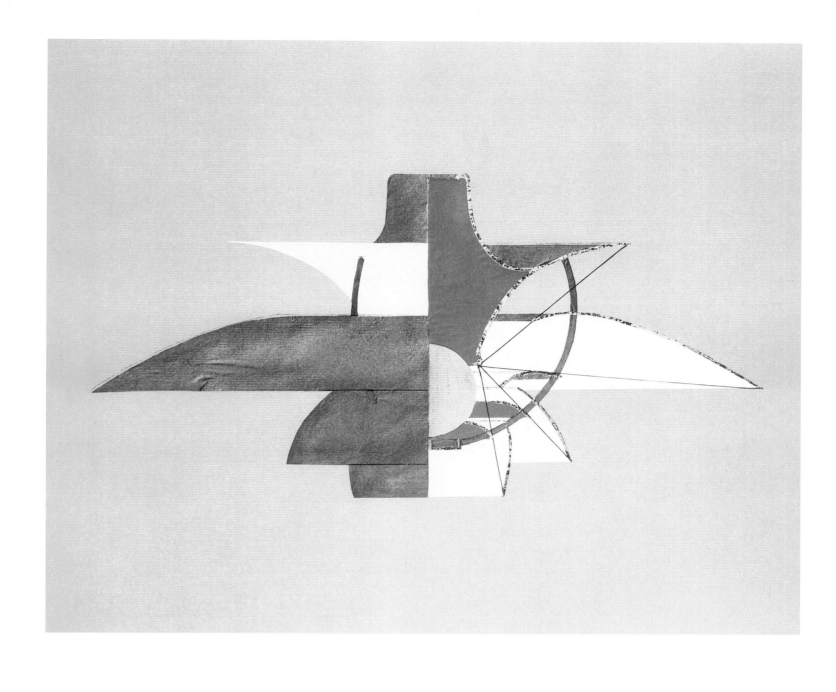

Opposite and above: Collages by Poul Henningsen's studio showing
the internal construction of his 1962 Contrast lamp (opposite) and the
1958 PH 5 lamp (above) for Louis Poulsen.

The Danish Museum of Decorative Art (now the Designmuseum Danmark) has a long-standing relationship with Louis Poulsen, and has showcased many of Henningsen's products over the years. It was there that the PH Septima[18] (see page 106) and the 1958 Snowball made their debut, the latter as part of a group exhibition titled *Glass, Light and Colour*.[19] A solo exhibition would come in 1994, opening on the centenary of Henningsen's birth on 9 September. *PH 100: Light and Design* demonstrated how Henningsen was Denmark's most significant lighting designer. It represented the first time that hundreds of Henningsen's designs were shown together, in their cultural and historical context. This seminal presentation traced Henningsen's career trajectory and considered lighting alongside his other pursuits, with a particular focus on his most productive years between the two World Wars.[20] Its curators were Tina Jørstian and Poul Erik Munk Nielsen, who in that same year edited the book *Light Years Ahead: The Story of the PH Lamp*, published by Louis Poulsen to highlight Henningsen's role in the evolution of light fittings.

Another comprehensive celebration of Henningsen's work took place from 2011 to 2012 at Koldinghus, a castle in the southern Danish town of Kolding. *PH Lamps: Poul Henningsen's Lighting Design 1924–2011* comprised 101 lamps from Louis Poulsen's collection, many of them recently acquired from a single collector.[21] Its exhibits ranged from his Paris lamp from 1925 all the way to a special edition of the Spiral lamp, with three spirals (in brass, copper and aluminium respectively) to enhance its dramatic effect, produced in 1967, the year of Henningsen's death. Visitors were likely to be familiar with the designer's better-known products, but would be encountering the rarer designs for the first time, such as a 1927 Septima, not yet reissued at the time;[22] a three-shade pendant in pleated paper, produced in 1943 amid material shortages; as well as a Smørrebrød lamp from 1965, intended for restaurant tables at the Hotel Marina, north of Copenhagen.[23] This lamp's three shades have a trio of supports piercing their perimeter (in addition to the tapering column at its centre), each capped with a ball screw so the lamp could support a platter of food. All of these lamps were illuminated in the vast Ruin Hall, 17 m (56 feet) high with 450-year-old brick surfaces deliberately left unrestored, amid the giant three-dimensional letters 'PH', a throwback to the 1934 Forum exhibition. Alongside, the exhibition also included more recent work by designers, both in Denmark and beyond, who cited Henningsen as their inspiration.[24]

In 2019, Tivoli staged the exhibition *Poul Henningsen in Tivoli* to mark the 125th anniversary of the designer's birth and tell the story of his partnership with the amusement park. Taking place at the Woodhouse café, this was a modest affair with around twenty historic lamps, but what it lacked in scale would have been made up for in footfall—as a spokesperson for the park explained, this was meant as an exhibition for 'both design nerds and the casually curious, which can be experienced on the go as part of a visit to Tivoli'.[25]

Above: Henningsen's 1965 Smørrebrød lamp for the Hotel Marina in Vedbæk, north of Copenhagen. Its trio of supports pierce through the shades and are each capped with a ball screw, so the lamp can support a platter of food.

Of course, Henningsen is not the only Louis Poulsen collaborator to be the subject of solo design exhibitions over the years—the 2000s saw a major Verner Panton retrospective organized by the Vitra Design Museum, which went on an impressive nine-year tour across Europe, the United States and East Asia and focused on furniture, although it also included the designer's lighting.[26] In 2021, the Trapholt Museum in Kolding would once again stage an extensive Panton presentation, titled *Colouring a New World*, introducing a new generation of audiences to the designer's work.[27] This followed the Trapholt exhibition *Arne Jacobsen—Designing Denmark*, which drew attention to lighting, textiles and design accessories alongside the well-trodden topics of his architecture and furniture.[28]

Opposite and above: Installation views of the *Arne Jacobsen—Designing Denmark* exhibition, which opened at the Trapholt Museum in Kolding, Denmark, in 2020 and drew attention to Jacobsen's lighting, textiles and design accessories, alongside his architecture and furniture. The Søllerød pendant, AJ Royal pendant and Aarhus City Hall pendant are seen opposite.

Such chronological and thematic presentations of the titans of mid-century Danish design reinforce our knowledge of their life and work and remind us of the role they played in shaping our world. But it is equally important to complement them with projects that encourage us to look at older designs in a new light, which is exactly the aim of the immersive exhibition *Louis Poulsen × Home in Heven*, staged in Copenhagen in 2023 during the annual *3daysofdesign* festival. The single-room installation was a collaboration with a pair of young glass artists and co-founders of hand-blown glass brand Heven, Breanna Box and Peter Dupont, who are based in Brooklyn. They created one-off remixes of classic Louis Poulsen designs—for example, a VL45 Radiohus pendant in pale pink, adorned with white tentacles that have blue glass beads representing suction cups, a PH table lamp with devil's horns, and a PH 2/2 Question Mark table lamp with pink shades that appear to have sprouted Saturn-like rings. These were displayed side by side with their original inspirations, albeit separated with one-way mirrors so the viewer could only see them when they crossed over to the other side of the installation. Following the exhibition, Louis Poulsen is planning to auction Heven's pieces in the United States, with most of the proceeds going to a youth charity that encourages access to the arts.[29]

Above: These one-off remixes of classic Louis Poulsen designs, by American-Danish duo Breanna Box and Peter Dupont of hand-blown glass brand Heven, debuted at Copenhagen's 3days*of*design festival in 2023 and will be auctioned for charity.

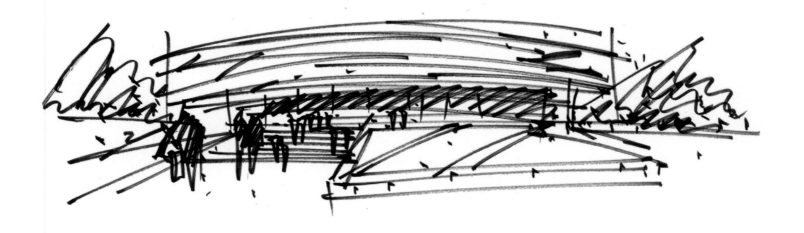

The Henningsen lamps that went on view at the Koldinghus exhibition still belong to the brand, and are being held in storage while they await a permanent home.[30] In 2010, Louis Poulsen expressed its hopes to create a new museum in Vejen, in the vicinity of its factory, to house this collection.[31] The proposed museum would present a holistic picture of Poul Henningsen, not only as a designer of light fixtures but also as a furniture designer, author, social critic and songwriter. It went so far as to commission Henning Larsen Architects to develop a design proposal. The announcement renderings showed a ring-shaped building amid lush greenery, with some similarities to a Foster + Partners later design for Apple Park in Cupertino, California. Its white horizontal louvres seemed to nod to Henningsen's Louvre pendant, a simplified, symmetrical variant of the Spiral lamp that he had created for Aarhus University. 'The round shape of the house creates a soft contrast to the rectangular geometry of the surrounding city,' read the accompanying text. 'As a large pavilion, the building rises from the ground, light as the clouds, poetic as Poul Henningsen himself.' Architectural statement aside, the proposed building was considered in its functionality, with

Above: Released in 2010, Henning Larsen Architects' rough sketch of a proposed Poul Henningsen Museum in Vejen, Denmark, in the vicinity of the Louis Poulsen factory. Plans for the museum have since been shelved.

a double-height atrium to facilitate the display of larger-scale pendants and lighting installations. The architects intended for Henningsen's works to be displayed along the inner facade, and created separate dark rooms to house special lighting exhibitions. There were also plans to include laboratories for the training of light technicians.[32]

The building cost would have to be raised from various foundations, with support from the Vejen Municipality. In the decade or so since, the plans have not materialized and Henning Larsen Architects has since taken down the project proposal from its website. One hopes, however, that given ongoing interest in Henningsen's work and his enduring influence on lighting design, there will eventually be a permanent exhibition to showcase his work, even if humbler in scale.

Considering the integral role that design and architecture have played in shaping Danish culture and heritage, it is surprising that there are not more such museums dedicated to its leading lights. The key exception, the Utzon Center in Aalborg, is worth considering as a blueprint: set in Jørn Utzon's final building, it has a permanent gallery dedicated to the architect's work, housing original sketches, models and digital presentations, but the bulk of the centre is dedicated to temporary exhibitions featuring contemporary architects, often with a focus on emerging talents. It is a suitable reflection of Utzon's forward-thinking character, and one imagines that a similar configuration would align with Henningsen's progressive views as well. Of course, a Henningsen exhibition could also go far in ensuring that his contributions to design, to our understanding of light and space, and indeed to Danish culture, continue to be acknowledged. But beyond lionizing Henningsen, a permanent exhibition would do well to include more recent and contemporary designs, and perhaps creative interpretations along the lines of Heven's artworks, to properly drive home how heritage designs continue to inspire, and how lighting design has evolved over the years, owing in large part to Louis Poulsen's legacy of innovation.

LOOKING AHEAD

So inventive and influential were the key players of mid-century Danish design that it is not easy to move out of their shadows. Indeed, there are some design brands in proud possession of a sizeable mid-century archive that seem burdened by the past, stuck in a cycle of reissues without being able to come up with an exciting new product. Then there are others that eagerly embrace the new without necessarily drawing a line between past and present, resulting in a somewhat disjointed catalogue. Happily, Louis Poulsen has managed to avoid both pitfalls. It has reissued archival pieces on a regular basis, working in close collaboration with the descendants of Henningsen, Jacobsen and the like to give fresh life and due attention to classic designs, without leaning on them entirely to define the brand. At the same time, since the early twenty first century, it has built an impressive roster of contemporary talents, who are immersed in the brand's long-standing design principles—particularly the lighting theories of Poul Henningsen—before being given the creative freedom and manufacturing support to chart their own course. In doing so, Louis Poulsen has not only reinforced its position as Denmark's first house of light, but also proven that the country has more to offer the world of design than the giants of modernism. New generations of designers have made their own mark with thoughtful products that leverage cutting-edge technologies, and their success is as much a reflection on their talent as on Louis Poulsen's continued ability to identify and nurture collaborators.

At the time of writing, Louis Poulsen is preparing its 150th anniversary celebrations, a landmark moment that will no doubt prompt some looking back. But this is just as apt a moment to look ahead, to consider the possibilities that lie with bolder sustainability initiatives that will follow on from the example of the PH 5 Retake, more experimental collaborations with nascent talents, along the lines of the SAGA Space Architects, one-off installations like Lise Vester's *Fabrikkens Idea Generator*, and further projects that blur the lines between art and design, be it the work of the next Anne Boysen or a whimsical historical reimagining in the mould of Heven's recent creations.

It is true that such projects may not have immediate commercial potential—as the original PH lamps did a century ago. But unlike Henningsen and his generation, today's designers are fortunate to live in an abundant society and need not envision a brave new world. Their task is to protect the one world we inhabit—by giving new life to existing products, and reconsidering our production systems to minimize their environmental impact—and to produce boundary-breaking work that helps us maintain our sense of awe and wonder in an era of sensory overload. By these measures, and considering its recent track record, Louis Poulsen is a business fit for the future. Long may it flourish.

Opposite: Louis Poulsen's Pale Rose collection, released in 2023, features iconic designs by Poul Henningsen and Vilhelm Lauritzen reinterpreted in pale rose opal glass with brass hardware.

Overleaf: Louis Poulsen's headquarters in Kuglegården, Copenhagen.

ENDNOTES

A BRIEF HISTORY

1   Lars Hedegaard, 'The First 125 Years', *LP Nyt,* no. 561 (1999); Ulf Ekman, 'Louis Poulsen & Co 100 år', *LP Nyt,* no. 380 (1973).
2   Tina Jørstian and Poul Erik Munk Nielsen, eds, *Light Years Ahead: The Story of the PH Lamp* (Copenhagen, 1994), p. 46.
3   Carl Erik Bay, 'Poul Henningsen', *Dansk Biografisk Leksikon* (accessed 24 July 2023), www.biografiskleksikon.lex.dk/Poul_Henningsen.
4   Jørstian and Munk Nielsen, *Light Years Ahead*, p. 47.
5   Ibid., pp. 76–8.
6   Ibid., pp. 86–8.
7   Ibid., pp. 66–73.
8   Ibid., pp. 102–3.
9   Ibid., pp. 103–116.
10 Ibid., pp. 118–19.
11 Ibid., p. 120; Jørgen Pedersen, 'Poul Henningsen's logarithmic spiral', *LP Nyt,* no. 567 (2000).
12 Malene Lytken, *Danish Lights—1920 to Now* (Copenhagen, 2019), pp. 38–9.
13 Jørstian and Munk Nielsen, *Light Years Ahead*, pp. 134–46.
14 Jørgen Pedersen, 'The PH lamp and its numbers', *LP Nyt,* no. 566 (2000).
15 Jørstian and Munk Nielsen, *Light Years Ahead*, pp. 146–150.
16 Hedegaard, 'The First 125 Years', p. 7.
17 Lytken, *Danish Lights*, pp. 38–9.
18 Hedegaard, 'The First 125 Years', pp. 8–9.
19 Jørstian and Munk Nielsen, *Light Years Ahead*, pp. 180–1.
20 Lars Dybdahl, ed., *101 Danish Design Icons* (Berlin, 2016), p. 61.
21 Jørstian and Munk Nielsen, *Light Years Ahead*, pp. 182–99.
22 Ibid., pp. 262–3.
23 Lytken, *Danish Lights—1920 to Now*, pp. 66–7.
24 Quoted in Ibid.
25 Ibid.; Jørstian and Munk Nielsen, *Light Years Ahead*, pp. 272–4; Stine Daugaard, 'Spot på PH's lamper i Kolding', *Ingeniøren* (30 March 2012), www.ing.dk/artikel/spot-paa-phs-lamper-i-kolding.
26 Quoted in Jørstian and Munk Nielsen, *Light Years Ahead*, pp. 266–8.
27 Author's visit to Designmuseum Danmark (22 June 2023).
28 Christie's, 'Poul Henningsen (1894–1967). A rare "Spiral" ceiling light': lot essay' (3 October 2017), www.christies.com/en/lot/lot-6101630.
29 Louis Poulsen, 'PH 5 pendant' (2018), www.louispoulsen.com/en-gb/catalog/private/pendants/ph-5.
30 Louis Poulsen, 'PH 2/2 Question Mark table lamp' (2021), www.louispoulsen.com/en-gb/catalog/private/table/ph-22-the-question-mark.
31 Louis Poulsen, 'Design to Shape Light' (2018), www.louispoulsen.com/en-gb/private/about-us/design-to-shape-light.
32 Hedegaard, 'The First 125 Years', p. 11.
33 Louis Poulsen, 'Our heritage', louispoulsen.com/en-gb/private/about-us/heritage.
34 Mirjam Gelfer-Jørgensen, *Influences from Japan in Danish Art and Design 1870–2010* (Copenhagen, 2013).
35 Louis Poulsen, 'NJP - Designed by nendo', YouTube (uploaded 3 January 2018), www.youtube.com/watch?v=h5iDIJo82Mg.
36 Author's interview with Søren Mygind Eskildsen (29 June 2023); Louis Poulsen, *Louis Poulsen Sustainability Report 2021* (Copenhagen, 2022) and *Louis Poulsen Sustainability Report 2022* (Copenhagen, 2023).
37 *Louis Poulsen Sustainability Report 2022.*
38 Creative Denmark, 'Louis Poulsen: A retake on the iconic PH 5' (25 October 2022), www.creativedenmark.com/cases/louis-poulsen-a-retake-on-the-iconic-ph-5; Louis Poulsen, 'PH 5 Retake', www.louispoulsen.com/en-gb/catalog/private/pendants/ph-5-retake.
39 Author's interview with Monique Faber (28 June 2023).

A SPIRIT OF DEMOCRACY

1   Phillips, '115. Poul Henningsen: Exceptional and large "Spiral" wall light, for the Scala cinema and concert hall, Århus Theater, Århus, Denmark' (17 November 2011), www.phillips.com/detail/poul-henningsen/UK050311/115.
2   Phillips, '114. Poul Henningsen: "The House of the Future" ceiling light' (17 November 2011), www.phillips.com/detail/poul-henningsen/UK050311/114.
3   Lars Dybdahl, ed., *101 Danish Design Icons* (Berlin, 2016), pp. 12–13.
4   Malene Lytken, *Danish Lights—1920 to Now* (Copenhagen, 2019), pp. 34–5.
5   Tina Jørstian and Poul Erik Munk Nielsen, eds, *Light Years Ahead: The Story of the PH Lamp* (Copenhagen, 1994), pp. 88–92; Louis Poulsen, 'PH: Philosophy of light', YouTube (3 videos of original documentary *PH lys*, 1964; uploaded 16 September 2008), www.youtube.com/watch?v=CFB4qgGTtMo, www.youtube.com/watch?v=t7nHqYzjYfw, www.youtube.com/watch?v=8ZpKg24_UKI.
6   Jørstian and Munk Nielsen, *Light Years Ahead*, pp. 120–30.
7   Ibid., p. 158.
8   Ibid., p. 156.
9   Author's visit to Aarhus Station (27 June 2023).
10 Alice Rawsthorn Instagram post, 'Design and light' (22 November 2016), www.instagram.com/p/BNGsBL9AZeA/?taken-by=alice.rawsthorn; Svend Erik Møller, Preben Willmann and Thomas Winding, eds, 'Til en afveksling har PH', *LP Nyt,* no. 273 (1964).
11 Robert McCarter, *Aalto* (London, 2014), p. 51.
12 Jørstian and Munk Nielsen, *Light Years Ahead*, pp. 210–15.
13 Ibid., pp. 231–3.
14 Koos Logger and Ingrid Stadler, 'The fascinating life of the PH Tennis Lamps at the K.B. Hallen in Copenhagen', Palainco (18 March 2019), www.palainco.com/discover/item/k-b-hallen-copenhagen-ph-tennis-lamps.
15 Carl Erik Bay, 'Poul Henningsen', *Dansk Biografisk Leksikon* (accessed 24 July 2023), www.biografiskleksikon.lex.dk/Poul_Henningsen.
16 Torben Jelsbak, 'From Bauhaus to Our House—*Kritisk Revy*, Popular Culture, and the Roots of "Scandinavian Design"', in Benedikt Hjartarson, et al., eds, *A Cultural History of the Avant-Garde in the Nordic Countries 1925–1950* (Leiden, 2019).
17 Dybdahl, *101 Danish Design Icons*, p. 63.
18 Jelsbak, 'From Bauhaus to Our House'.
19 Dybdahl, *101 Danish Design Icons*, p. 65.
20 Møller, Willmann and Winding, 'Til en afveksling har PH'.
21 Bay, 'Poul Henningsen'; Alice Rawsthorn Instagram post, 'Poul Henningsen' (4–10 September 2020), www.instagram.com/p/BYm8AfzAeYt/?taken-by=alice.rawsthorn.

22 Jørstian and Munk Nielsen, *Light Years Ahead*, pp. 24–7; C. Claire Thomson, 'Lamps, Light, and Enlightenment: Poul Henningsen's Denmark and Ole Roos' PH Light', *Kosmorama* (31 May 2013), www.kosmorama.org/en/kosmorama/artikler/lamps-light-and-enlightenment-poul-henningsens-denmark-and-ole-roos-ph-light.

23 Author's interview with Charlotte June Henningsen, Peter Johansen and Louise Danneskiold-Samsøe (28 June 2023).

24 Anders V. Munch, 'Conspicuously Quotidian: Poul Henningsen on Bauhaus and the Art of Promoting Danish Modern', *Tahiti* (2021), www.tahiti.journal.fi/article/view/111940/65714, p. 12.

25 Bay, 'Poul Henningsen'.

26 Lars Hedegaard, 'The First 125 Years', *LP Nyt*, no. 561 (1999), pp. 37–8; Rawsthorn, 'Poul Henningsen'.

27 Pia Buhl Andersen, 'Nazigruppe ville dræbe dansk stjernearkitekt', *Politiken* (13 October 2012), www.politiken.dk/kultur/art5411366/Nazigruppe-ville-dr%C3%A6be-dansk-stjernearkitekt.

28 Hedegaard, 'The First 125 Years', pp. 37–8.

29 Hans Hertel, *Good Light* (Copenhagen, 2016).

30 Author's interview with Ellen Dahl (28 June 2023).

31 Tivoli, 'The History of Tivoli', www.tivoli.dk/en/om/tivolis-historie.

32 Ellen Dahl (28 June 2023).

33 Ben Hamilton, 'Remembering Tivoli's founder: a showman with a fondness for champagne and jazzy waistcoats', *CPH Post* (23 May 2017), www.cphpost.dk/2017-05-23/history/tivoli.

34 Edwin G. Burrows, *The Finest Building in America: The New York Crystal Palace 1853–1858* (New York, 2018), p. 36.

35 Eleanor Beardsley, 'Tivoli Gardens Beckons on Denmark's Summer Nights', NPR (15 August 2012), www.npr.org/2012/08/15/158870832/on-denmarks-summer-nights-tivoli-gardens-beckon.

36 Ellen Dahl (28 June 2023).

37 Ibid.

38 Jørstian and Munk Nielsen, *Light Years Ahead*, pp. 255–7.

39 Author's visit to the Danish Architecture Center (4 July 2023).

40 Lytken, *Danish Lights*, pp. 62–3.

41 Quoted in Ida Præstegaard, 'The PH lamps in Tivoli Gardens are rotating again', *LP Nyt*, no. 586 (2008).

42 Ibid.

43 Author's visit to Tivoli (28 June 2023).

44 Author's interview with Louise Campbell (12 July 2023).

45 Tivoli press release, 'Poul Henningsen in Tivoli: Exhibition Marks 125th Anniversary of Poul Henningsen's Birth' (22 January 2019), www.tivoli.dk/en/om/presse/pressemeddelelser/2019/ph-i-tivoli-udstilling.

46 Louis Poulsen, 'PH in Tivoli', *Reflections*, no. 6 (2019), www.catalogue.louispoulsen.com/UK/louis-poulsen-reflections-6/.

47 Jørstian and Munk Nielsen, *Light Years Ahead*, pp. 288–92.

48 Louis Poulsen, 'PH: Philosophy of light'.

49 Ibid.

50 Author's interview with Christian Flindt (11 July 2023).

51 Hedegaard, 'The First 125 Years', pp. 10–11.

52 Ibid., p. 13.

53 Sverre Riis Christensen, 'A Real Advertising Tale', *LP Nyt*, no. 561 (1999).

54 Jørstian and Munk Nielsen, *Light Years Ahead*, pp. 281–2; Lytken, *Danish Lights*, pp. 78–9.

55 Dybdahl, *101 Danish Design Icons*, p. 61.

56 Dansk Møbeldesign, 'Udstilling om PH lamper på Koldinghus' (2012), www.danskmoebeldesign.dk/udstilling-om-ph-lamper-paa-koldinghus.html.

57 Author's interview with Monique Faber (28 June 2023).

58 Louis Poulsen, 'Cirque' (2016), www.louispoulsen.com/en-gb/catalog/private/pendants/cirque.

59 Louis Poulsen, 'PH: Philosophy of light'.

60 Alison Flood, 'Terry Pratchett estate backs Jack Monroe's idea for "Vimes Boots" poverty index', *Guardian* (26 January 2022), www.theguardian.com/books/2022/jan/26/terry-pratchett-jack-monroe-vimes-boots-poverty-index.

61 Lytken, *Danish Lights*, pp. 86–7.

62 Holger Dahl, 'Arkens nye udendørs trækplaster er »ganske enkelt fremragende«', *Berlingske* (27 June 2021), www.berlingske.dk/design-mode-og-arkitektur/arkens-nye-udendoers-traekplaster-er-ganske-enkelt.

63 Danske Litteraturpriser ved Niels Jensen, 'PH Prisen', www.litteraturpriser.dk/divkult.htm#PH.

64 Louis Poulsen, 'Sophus Fonden', www.louispoulsen.com/da-dk/private/om-os/sophusfonden.

65 SAGA Space Architects press release, 'LUNARK—Building and Testing a Moon Home for Everyone', (2020), www.docs.google.comdocument/d/16eq25FRlyGlqHEtbNsfrYTeUn2wQF4imJeLtULtlwj0.

66 SAGA Space Architects, 'LUNARK—Louis Poulsen', Vimeo (uploaded 5 May 2021), www.vimeo.com/545503755.

67 Ibid.

68 Ibid.

69 Ibid.

70 Utzon Center, 'A Space Saga: Mar 31st 2023 to Sep 3rd 2023' (2023), www.utzoncenter.dk/enexhibition/a-space-saga-10346.

71 London Design Biennale, 'Denmark & Switzerland: Blue Nomad' (2023), www.londondesignbiennale.com/pavilions/2023/denmark-switzerland.

72 Lise Vester, 'About—Lise Vester', www.lisevester.dk.

73 Lise Vester 'Lise Vester Studio 2022', YouTube (uploaded 10 May 2022), www.youtube.com/watch?v=r9VskD6GBbY.

74 Lise Vester Instagram post, 'The Making of Fabrikkens Idea Generator' (11 October 2022), www.instagram.com/p/CjkWBmXjUSM.

75 3daysofdesign news post, 'Bo Bedre's Design Awards 2022' (2022), www.3daysofdesign.dk/post/bo-bedres-design-awards-2022.

THE PH ARTICHOKE

1 Wava Carpenter, 'The Perennial Artichoke: Peeling back the layers of Poul Henningsen's timeless design', Pamono (2 February 2016), www.pamono.com/stories/poul-henningsen-artichoke-lamp-story.

2 Malene Lytken, *Danish Lights—1920 to Now* (Copenhagen, 2019), front cover image.

3 Chris Chapman, 'Hall of Fame', *Wallpaper** (January/February 1998).

4 Hannah Martin, 'The Story Behind the Revolutionary Artichoke Light', *Architectural Digest* (30 June 2018), www.architecturaldigest.com/story/the-story-behind-the-revolutionary-artichoke-light.

5 Paula Benson, 'Lights and lamps inspiration from film and TV', Film and Furniture (6 July 2022), www.filmandfurniture.com/2022/07/lights-and-lamps-inspiration-from-film-and-tv/.

6   John Heward, 'Langeliniepavillonen / The Langelinie Pavilion', Danish Design Review (4 December 2018), www.danishdesignreview.com/kbhnotes/2018/12/12/langeliniepavillonen-the-langelinie-pavilion; Martin Keiding and Kim Dirckinck-Holmfeld, *Utzon and the New Tradition* (Copenhagen, 2005), p. 56.

7   Ida Præstegaard, 'The first PH Artichokes are still there', *LP Nyt*, no. 572 (2002).

8   Ibid.

9   Lytken, *Danish Lights*, pp. 68–9.

10 Tina Jørstian and Poul Erik Munk Nielsen, eds, *Light Years Ahead: The Story of the PH Lamp* (Copenhagen, 1994), pp. 237–9.

11 Louis Poulsen, 'PH Septima' (2020), www.louispoulsen.com/en-gb/catalog/private/pendants/ph-septima.

12 Jørstian and Munk Nielsen, eds, *Light Years Ahead*, pp. 237–9; author's interview with Kristine Stilling Pedersen (27 June 2023).

13 Quoted in Præstegaard, 'The first PH Artichokes are still there'.

14 Lytken, *Danish Lights*, pp. 68–9.

15 Kristine Stilling Pedersen (27 June 2023).

16 George Hammond, 'Design classic: PH Artichoke lamp', *Financial Times* (23 March 2018), www.ft.com/content/793f91d4-2798-11e8-9274-2b13fccdc744.

17 Mark Mussari, *Danish Modern: Between Art and Design* (London, 2016).

18 Michael Sheridan, *The Furniture of Poul Kjærholm: Catalogue Raisonné* (New York, 2007), p. 14.

19 Cindi Strauss, 'Poul Henningsen', in Sarah Schleuning and Cindi Strauss, eds, *Electrifying Design: A Century of Lighting* (Houston, 2021).

20 Louis Poulsen, 'PH Artichoke Glass' (2012), www.louispoulsen.com/en-gb/catalog/private/pendants/ph-artichoke-glass.

21 Author's interviews with Kristine Stilling Pedersen, and Lisbeth Mansfeldt (28 June 2023).

22 Author's interview with Søren Mygind Eskildsen (29 June 2023).

23 'Danes tend to consider extravagance immoral'. Quoted in Ida Præstegaard, 'Light must be honest: Interview with Mads Odgård', *LP Lyt*, no. 574 (2003).

24 Mairi Beautyman, 'Louis Poulsen Celebrates 60 Years with a Limited-Edition PH Artichoke Lamp', *Architectural Digest* (1 June 2018), www.architecturaldigest.com/story/louis-poulsen-poul-henningsen-artichoke-lamp-60-years.

25 Louis Poulsen, 'PH Artichoke' (2018), www.louispoulsen.com/en-gb/catalog/private/pendants/ph-artichoke.

26 Louis Poulsen, 'PH Artichoke Pale Rose' (2023), www.louispoulsen.com/en-gb/catalog/private/pendants/ph-artichoke-pale-rose.

27 Louis Poulsen, 'The PH Artichoke's new little brother', *LP Nyt*, no. 572 (2002).

28 Patrick Kingsley, *How to Be Danish: A Journey to the Cultural Heart of Denmark* (London, 2012), p. 46.

29 Oda Collection, '織田邸の暮らし―Life at Oda's Residence, Vol. 6 織田憲嗣スペシャルインタビュー―Noritsugu Oda's Special Interview', YouTube (uploaded 1 February 2022), www.youtube.com/watch?v=CVcUXsSWgP0.

30 Author's interview with Yoichi Nishio (19 September 2023).

31 Natasha Garnett, 'Italian Modern: The Gallerist Nina Yashar', *New York Times* (29 October 2014), www.nytimes.com/2014/10/29/t-magazine/italian-modern.html.

32 Thimo Te Duits, ed., *The Origin of Things: Sketches, Models, Prototypes* (Rotterdam, 2003), p. 122.

33 &Tradition, 'Langelinie Pavilion, Restaurant & Events' (2020), www.andtradition.com/journal/langelinie-pavilion.

34 Alex Ronan, 'The Lighting Fixture that Inspired a High-Stakes Heist: The PH Artichoke', *Dwell* (15 February 2015), www.dwell.com/article/the-lighting-fixture-that-inspired-a-high-stakes-heist-the-ph-artichoke-7aa5d797.

35 Bonhams, 'Lot 46W. Poul Henningsen (1894–1967): Important Pre-Production Artichoke Ceiling Light from the Langelinie Pavilion' (2018), www.bonhams.com/auction/24848/lot/46/poul-henningsen-1894-1967-important-pre-production-artichoke-ceiling-light-from-the-langelinie-pavilion1958for-louis-poulsen-solid-copper-nickel-plated-brass-pale-pink-reflective-interior-paint-plastic-top-plate-engraved-lpheight-26in-66cm-diameter-31in-79cm/.

36 Louis Poulsen, 'PH Reflections: Louise Campbell', *Reflections*, no. 3 (2018), p. 61, www.catalogue.louispoulsen.com/UK/louis-poulsen-reflections-3.

THE CRADLE OF MODERNISM

1   Louis Poulsen, 'Arne Jacobsen' (2018), www.louispoulsen.com/en-gb/private/about-us/designers/arne-jacobsen.

2   Arne Jacobsen Design, 'Authorized Partners' (2022), www.arnejacobsen.com/authenticity/authorized-partners.

3   Arne Jacobsen Design, 'House of the Future' (2022), www.arnejacobsen.com/works/house-of-the-future/.

4   Malene Lytken, *Danish Lights—1920 to Now* (Copenhagen, 2019), pp. 42–3.

5   Danish Architecture Center, 'Stellings Hus: Undiscovered Icon on the Oldest Square in Copenhagen' (18 June 2021), www.dac.dk/en/knowledgebase/architecture/stellings-hus-stelling-house-undiscovered-icon-on-the-oldest-square-in-copenhagen/.

6   Carsten Thau and Kjeld Vindum, *Arne Jacobsen* (Copenhagen, 1998), pp. 256, 264, 292.

7   Ibid., p. 292.

8   Ibid., p. 307.

9   Arne Jacobsen Design, 'SAS Royal Hotel' (2022), www.arnejacobsen.com/works/sas-royal-hotel.

10 Arne Jacobsen Design, 'AJ Lamp' (2022), www.arnejacobsen.com/works/aj-lamp; Lytken, *Danish Lights*, pp. 64–5.

11 Louis Poulsen, 'AJ Table' (2018), www.louispoulsen.com/en-gb/catalog/private/table/aj-table.

12 Lytken, *Danish Lights*, pp. 64–5.

13 Louis Poulsen, 'AJ Royal' (2020), www.louispoulsen.com/en-gb/catalog/private/pendants/aj-royal.

14 Louis Poulsen, 'Munkegaard' (2019), www.louispoulsen.com/en/catalog/professional/architectural-lighting/recessed/munkegaard.

15 Louis Poulsen, 'AJ Eklipta' (2014), www.louispoulsen.com/en-gb/catalog/private/wall/aj-eklipta.

16 Louis Poulsen, 'AJ Oxford Table Lamp' (2023), www.louispoulsen.com/en-gb/catalog/private/table/aj-oxford-table-lamp.

17 Rosa Bertoli, 'Arne Jacobsen's lamps for St Catherine's College are now available from Louis Poulsen', *Wallpaper** (25 February 2023), www.wallpaper.com/design-interiors/arne-jacobsen-saint-catherine-college-cambridge-lamps-louis-poulsen.

18 Author's interview with Monique Faber (29 June 2023).

19 Christian Bundegaard, *100 Years of Danish Modern: Vilhelm Lauritzen Architects* (Copenhagen, 2022), pp. 242–3.

20 Louis Poulsen, 'Vilhelm Lauritzen' (2018), www.louispoulsen.com/en-gb/private/about-us/designers/vilhelm-lauritzen.

21 Quoted in Lytken, *Danish Lights*, pp. 50–1.

22 Dansk Møbelkunst, 'Vilhelm Lauritzen: "Universal" Pendant' (2021), www.dmk.dk/item/vilhelm-lauritzen-the-universal-pendant-1929-louis-poulsen/.

23 Vilhelm Lauritzen Architects, 'The Radio House' (2022), www.vilhelmlauritzen.com/project/radiohouse.

24 Lytken, *Danish Lights*, pp. 50–1.

25 Louis Poulsen, 'VL 38 Table' (2016), www.louispoulsen.com/en-gb/catalog/private/table/vl38-table.

26 Louis Poulsen, 'VL Studio' (2022), www.louispoulsen.com/en-gb/catalog/professional/decorative-lighting/floor/vl-studio-tablefloor.

27 Lytken, *Danish Lights*, pp. 50–1.

28 Reinhard Krause, 'Leuchtendes Beispiel: Vilhelm Lauritzen und seine ikonischen Möbel', *Architectural Digest Deutschland* (1 December 2011), www.ad-magazin.de/article/ikone-vilhelm-lauritzen.

29 Louis Poulsen, 'VL Studio'.

30 House of Finn Juhl, 'Timeline' (2022), www.finnjuhl.com/about/timeline.

31 Lytken, *Danish Lights*, pp. 52–3.

32 Visavu, 'Vilhelm Lauritzen pair of Guldpendel lamps, Denmark 1955' (2020), www.visavu.nl/portfolio/vilhelm-lauritzen-pair-of-guldpendel-lamps-denmark-1955/.

33 Louis Poulsen, 'VL 56 Pendant' (2023), www.louispoulsen.com/en/catalog/private/pendants/vl-56-pendant.

34 Alan De Waal, 'Lighting Culture', *LP Nyt*, no. 561 (1999).

35 Vilhelm Lauritzen and Poul Henningsen, 'Idealisme og honorar', *LP Nyt*, no. 110 (1951).

36 Artek, 'Pendant Light A330S "Golden Bell"' (2018), www.artek.fi/en/products/pendant-light-a330s-golden-bell; Savoy Helsinki, 'Savoy Restaurant' (2020), www.savoyhelsinki.fi/restaurant.

37 North Sea Design, 'MK 114 Mogens Koch In-light Pendant Lamp' [year unknown], www.northseadesign.nl/en/mk-114-mogens-koch-pendant.html; In-Light Scandinavia, 'Mogens Koch' (2020), www.in-light.dk/designre/mogens-koch.

38 Michael Sheridan, *Louisiana: Architecture and Landscape* (Humlebæk, 2017), pp. 86, 101, 109; TF Chan, 'Own a piece of classic Danish furniture as seen in the Louisiana Museum of Modern Art' (22 August 2018), www.wallpaper.com/design/louisiana-museum-of-modern-art-60th-anniversary-reissues.

39 Lytken, *Danish Lights*, pp. 70–1.

40 Louis Poulsen, 'Wohlert Pendant' (2018), www.louispoulsen.com/en/catalog/private/pendants/wohlert-790ab121.

41 Murray Moss, *Georg Jensen: Reflections* (New York, 2014), pp. 142–5.

42 Lytken, *Danish Lights*, pp. 82–3.

43 1stDibs, 'Henning Koppel Pewter Vase for Georg Jensen' (2021), 1stdibs.com/en-gb/furniture/decorative-objects/vases-vessels/vases/henning-koppel-pewter-vase-georg-jensen.

44 Lytken, *Danish Lights*, pp. 82–3.

45 Ibid., pp. 128–9.

46 Moss, *Georg Jensen*, pp. 142–5.

47 Lytken, *Danish Lights*, pp. 136–7; Dansk Møbelkunst, 'Hans J. Wegner table lamp for Aarhus City Hall' (2022), www.dmk.dk/item/hans-wegner-table-lamp-aarhus-city-hall/.

48 Lytken, *Danish Lights*, pp. 76–7. The design was produced by cabinetmaker Johannes Hansen before being taken over by Louis Poulsen.

49 Ibid., pp. 136–7.

50 Okholm Lighting, 'Wegnerlygten' (2019), www.okholm-lighting.dk/produkter-visning/udendorsbelysning/wegnerlygten.

51 Ida Engholm and Anders Michelsen, *Verner Panton* (London, 2018), pp. 23–5.

52 Lytken, *Danish Lights*, pp. 72–3.

53 Engholm and Michelsen, *Verner Panton*, p. 28.

54 Ibid., p. 327.

55 Lytken, *Danish Lights*, pp. 72–3; Engholm and Michelsen, *Verner Panton*, pp. 28–9.

56 Lytken, *Danish Lights*, pp. 98–9.

57 Adam Christopher Design, 'Design Classic 1960 Verner Panton the Moon Pendant Review', YouTube (uploaded 23 August 2017), www.youtube.com/watch?v=vAYRAmGtXuM.

58 Ibid.

59 Engholm and Michelsen, *Verner Panton*, pp. 156–7.

60 Lytken, *Danish Lights*, pp. 106–7.

61 Engholm and Michelsen, *Verner Panton*, pp. 180–1.

62 Lytken, *Danish Lights*, pp. 110–11.

63 Alan De Waal, 'Panton's Universe', *LP Nyt*, no. 562 (1999); Engholm and Michelsen, *Verner Panton*, p. 229.

64 *LP Nyt*, no. 355 (1971).

65 Quoted in Lytken, *Danish Lights*, pp. 112–13; Engholm and Michelsen, *Verner Panton*, p. 237.

66 De Waal, 'Panton's Universe'.

67 Lytken, *Danish Lights*, pp. 122–3; Monique Faber (29 June 2023).

68 Ibid.

69 Louis Poulsen, 'Panthella 160 Portable' (2022), www.louispoulsen.com/en-gb/catalog/private/table/panthella-160-portable.

CRAFT AND TECHNOLOGY

1 Robert Friedel and Paul B. Israel, *Edison's Electric Light: The Art of Invention* (Baltimore, 2010), p. 81.

2 Diane Bailey, *How the Light Bulb Changed History* (North Mankato, Minn., 2015), p. 24.

3 Science History Institute, 'Critical Metals: The Chemistry of Light', Google Arts & Culture (2022), www.artsandculture.google.com/story/critical-metals-the-chemistry-of-light-science-history-institute/9AWhIBWIbZ1jUQ.

4 Ainissa Ramirez, 'Tungsten's Brilliant, Hidden History', *American Scientist* (27 January 2020), www.americanscientist.org/article/tungstens-brilliant-hidden-history.

5 Tina Jørstian and Poul Erik Munk Nielsen, eds, *Light Years Ahead: The Story of the PH Lamp* (Copenhagen, 1994), pp. 67–8.

6 Ibid., p. 62.

7 Sandy Isenstadt, *Electric Light: An Architectural History* (Cambridge, Mass., 2018), p. 19.

8 Louis Poulsen, 'PH: Philosophy of light', YouTube (one of three videos of original documentary *PH lys*, 1964; uploaded 16 September 2008), www.youtube.com/watch?v=CFB4qgGTtMo.

9 Malene Lytken, *Danish Lights—1920 to Now* (Copenhagen, 2019), pp. 23–4.

10 Mogens Voltelen, 'PH lampen i histories belysning', *LP Nyt*, no. 112 (1951).

11 Jørstian and Munk Nielsen, *Light Years Ahead*, pp. 272–6; Lytken, *Danish Lights*, pp. 66–7.

12 Dansk Møbelkunst, 'An extraordinary PH lamp' (31 January 2020), www.dmk.dk/the-fluorescent-pendant-ph/.

13 Lytken, *Danish Lights*, p. 30; Bailey, *How the Light Bulb Changed History*, p. 85.

14 Lytken, *Danish Lights*, p. 30.

15 Arthur Nelsen, 'Europe to ban halogen lightbulbs', *Guardian* (23 August 2018), www.theguardian.com/environment/2018/aug/23/europe-to-ban-halogen-lightbulbs.

16   Hiroko Tabuchi, 'It's Official: Stores Can No Longer Sell Most Incandescent Lights', *New York Times* (1 August 2023), www.nytimes.com/2023/08/01/climate/incandescent-light-bulb-ban-leds.html.

17   Jaehee Cho, et al., 'White light-emitting diodes: History, progress, and future', *Laser & Photonics Reviews* (2 March 2017), www.onlinelibrary.wiley.com/doi/10.1002/lpor.201600147.

18   Arlene Hirst, 'As Traditional Bulbs Fade Out, LED Lights Keep Improving', *New York Times* (3 May 2023), www.nytimes.com/2023/05/03/style/led-lights-improving.html.

19   Jørstian and Munk Nielsen, *Light Years Ahead*, pp. 281–2; author's interview with Lisbeth Mansfeldt (5 July 2023).

20   Jørstian and Munk Nielsen, *Light Years Ahead*, pp. 174–5.

21   Ibid., pp. 266–7.

22   Ibid., p. 274.

23   Lytken, *Danish Lights*, pp. 72–3; twentytwentyone, 'Moon Pendant, 1960' (2020), www.twentytwentyone.com/products/verpan-verner-panton-moon.

24   Lytken, *Danish Lights,* pp. 64–5. The retail edition of the AJ pendant was originally made in lacquered aluminium. Today all AJ lamps are made in lacquered steel.

25   Ibid., pp. 62–3.

26   Ibid., pp. 114–15.

27   Ibid., pp. 122–3.

28   Ida Engholm and Anders Michelsen, *Verner Panton*, pp. 110–11; 'Verner Panton', *Domus* (2021), www.domusweb.it/en/biographies/verner-panton.html.

29   Lytken, *Danish Lights*, pp. 136–7.

30   Ida Præstegaard, 'From unconventional idea to reality', *LP Nyt,* no. 581 (2005).

31   Jørstian and Munk Nielsen, *Light Years Ahead*, pp. 124, 180–1.

32   Ulf Ekman, 'Louis Poulsen & Co 100 år', *LP Nyt,* no. 380 (1973).

33   Fred Madsen, 'Louis Poulsen tænder nyt lys i Vejen', *Berlingske* (13 April 2005), www.berlingske.dk/business/louis-poulsen-taender-nyt-lys-i-vejen.

34   Author's interview with Kristine Stilling Pedersen (27 June 2023).

35   Kasper Iversen, 'PH-lampen: Fra politisk statement til sikkert valg', *Politiken* (3 April 2015), www.politiken.dk/kultur/design/art5572179/PH-lampen-Fra-politisk-statement-til-sikkert-valg.

36   Lytken, *Danish Lights*, pp. 146–7.

37   As observed on the author's visit to Louis Poulsen factory (27 June 2023).

38   Ibid.

INTO THE PRESENT

1   Author's interview with Lisbeth Mansfeldt (28 June 2023).

2   Emma O'Kelly, 'Great Dane', *Wallpaper** (April 2001).

3   Malene Lytken, *Danish Lights—1920 to Now* (Copenhagen, 2019), pp. 148–9.

4   Louis Poulsen, 'Alfred Homann' (2019), www.louispoulsen.com/en-gb/private/about-us/designers/alfred-homann.

5   Lytken, *Danish Lights*, pp. 158–9.

6   Author's interview with Ulla Riemer (12 July 2023).

7   Ibid.

8   Author's interview with Louise Campbell (12 July 2023).

9   Tina Jørstian and Poul Erik Munk Nielsen, eds, *Light Years Ahead: The Story of the PH Lamp* (Copenhagen, 1994), pp. 237–9.

10   Lytken, *Danish Lights*, pp. 170–1.

11   Louise Poulsen, 'Campbell Pendant', *LP Nyt,* no. 579 (2004).

12   Lytken, *Danish Lights*, pp. 170–1.

13   Ida Præstegaard, 'From unconventional idea to reality', *LP Nyt,* no. 581 (2005).

14   Lytken, *Danish Lights*, pp. 180–1.

15   Louis Poulsen, 'LC Shutters—Pendant by Louise Campbell', YouTube (uploaded 1 March 2012), www.youtube.com/watch?v=4bUg5T8hVcE.

16   Catherine Lazure-Guinard, 'LC Shutters by Louise Campbell', Nordic Design (27 February 2012), www.nordicdesign.ca/lc-shutters-by-louise-campbell/.

17   Ulla Riemer (12 July 2023).

18   Author's interview with Monique Faber (28 June 2023).

19   Caroline Roux, 'Prism Break: Louise Campbell's "Nervous" chandelier for Baccarat pushed both designer and manufacturer to the limit', *Wallpaper** (May 2013).

20   Louise Campbell (12 July 2023).

21   Author's interview with Christian Flindt (11 July 2013).

22   Louis Poulsen, 'New Fixtures in Light and Unpretentious Design', *LP Nyt,* no. 585 (2007).

23   Louis Poulsen, 'Flindt Garden Bollard' (2020), www.louispoulsen.com/en-gb/catalog/private/outdoor/flindt-garden-bollard.

24   Louis Poulsen, 'Spotlight on Christian Flindt', *Reflections,* no. 4 (2018).

25   Author's interview with Øivind Slaatto (5 July 2023); Be Original Americas and Louis Poulsen, 'Be Original Americas × Louis Poulsen: Conversation with Øivind Slaatto', YouTube (uploaded 29 July 2020), www.youtube.com/watch?v=-4KWgkN5qUo.

26   Louis Poulsen, 'Øivind Slaatto's Patera Silver', *Reflections,* no. 5 (2019).

27   Louis Poulsen, 'PH Reflections: Øivind Slaatto', *Reflections,* no. 3 (2018), p. 63, www.catalogue.louispoulsen.com/UK/louis-poulsen-reflections-3.

28   Louis Poulsen, 'Patera' (2018), www.louispoulsen.com/en-gb/catalog/private/pendants/patera.

29   Øivind Slaatto (5 July 2023).

30   Louis Poulsen, 'Patera'.

31   Louis Poulsen, 'Øivind Slaatto's Patera Silver'; Lytken, *Danish Lights*, pp. 206–7.

32   Louis Poulsen, 'Patera Oval' (2021), www.louispoulsen.com/en-gb/catalog/private/pendants/patera-oval.

33   Author interview with Kristine Stilling Pedersen (27 June 2023).

34   Author interview with Yoichi Nishio (19 September 2023).

35   Ida Præstegaard, 'Enigma', *LP Nyt,* no. 576 (2003).

36   Uchiyama Design, 'Enigma 425 White/Black' [year unknown], www.uchiyama-design.jp/works/enigma425.html.

37   Ulla Riemer (12 July 2023).

38   Danielle Demetriou, '5x5: Nendo', *Wallpaper** (October 2021).

39   nendo, 'NJP table' (2015), www.nendo.jp/en/works/njp-table-2/.

40   Louis Poulsen, 'NJP—Designed by nendo', YouTube (uploaded 3 January 2018), www.youtube.com/watch?v=h5iDlJo82Mg.

41   Author's interview with Mads Odgård (3 July 2023); Louis Poulsen, 'Above' (2018), www.louispoulsen.com/en-gb/catalog/private/pendants/above-pendant.

42   Louis Poulsen, 'Thoughts about Cirque—Designed by Clara von Zweigbergk—Produced by Louis Poulsen', YouTube (uploaded 23 March 2018), www.youtube.com/watch?v=Rvwfe4uqF8w.

43   Lizzie Fison, 'Clara von Zweigbergk's colourful lamps recall hot air balloons and carousels' (2 June 2017), www.dezeen.com/2017/06/02/clara-von-zweigbergk-louis-poulsen-colourful-lamps-hot-air-balloons-carousels/.

44   Louis Poulsen, 'A Lamp is Born', *Reflections,* no. 2 (2017).

45   Louis Poulsen, 'Yuh Table' (2018), www.louispoulsen.com/en-gb/
      catalog/private/table/yuh-table.
46   Louis Poulsen, 'A Lamp is Born'.
47   Lytken, *Danish Lights*, pp. 216–7.
48   Jørstian and Munk Nielsen, *Light Years Ahead*, pp. 60–1.
49   Lisbeth Bonde, 'Serial Lighting: 60 years of *Nyt*', *LP Nyt*,
      no. 570 (2001).
50   Alyn Griffiths, 'Cosmic rays: Artist Olafur Eliasson scales down,
      shapes up and finds an inner light', *Wallpaper** (May 2019).
51   Peter Schjeldahl, 'Uncluttered: An Olafur Eliasson retrospective',
      New Yorker (21 April 2008),
      www.newyorker.com/magazine/2008/04/28/uncluttered.
52   Studio Olafur Eliasson, 'The weather project, 2003' (2023),
      www.olafureliasson.net/artwork/the-weather-project-2003/.
53   Studio Other Spaces, www.studiootherspaces.net.
54   Lytken, *Danish Lights*, pp. 168–9.
55   Studio Olafur Eliasson, 'Ice Watch, 2014' (2023),
      www.olafureliasson.net/artwork/ice-watch-2014/.
56   Little Sun, 'Mission—Little Sun' (2022), www.littlesun.org/about/
      mission/.
57   Griffiths, 'Cosmic rays'.
58   Monique Faber (28 June 2023).
59   Author's interview with Søren Mygind Eskildsen (29 June 2023).
60   Griffiths, 'Cosmic rays'.
61   Monique Faber (28 June 2023).
62   Lytken, *Danish Lights*, pp. 228–9.
63   Anne Boysen, 'Moonsetter', www.anneboysen.dk/#/moonsetter-
      louis-poulsen/; Ryan Waddoups, 'Designer of the Day: Anne
      Boysen', *Surface* (19 December 2022), www.surfacemag.com/
      articles/anne-boysen-designer-day/.
64   Louis Poulsen, 'Moonsetter' (2021), www.louispoulsen.com/en-
      gb/catalog/private/floor/moonsetter.
65   Waddoups, 'Designer of the Day: Anne Boysen'.
66   Ibid.
67   Monique Faber (28 June 2023).
68   Louis Poulsen, 'PH Septima: Finding a Lost Icon', *Reflections*,
      no. 8 (2020).
69   Author's interview with Anne Boysen (5 July 2023).
70   Christian Flindt (11 July 2023).

HOME AND BEYOND

1   Tina Jørstian and Poul Erik Munk Nielsen, eds, *Light Years
      Ahead: The Story of the PH Lamp* (Copenhagen, 1994), p. 208.
2   Ibid., pp. 212–13.
3   Sverre Riis Christensen, 'A Real Advertising Tale', *LP Nyt*,
      no. 561 (1999).
4   Ibid.; Lisbeth Bonde, 'Serial Lighting: 60 years of *Nyt*', *LP Nyt*,
      no. 570 (2001).
5   Ibid.
6   Bonde, 'Serial Lighting: 60 years of *Nyt*'.
7   Noriyuki Asakura, 'Japanese Light', *LP Nyt*, no. 559 (1998).
8   Louis Poulsen, 'Louis Poulsen Learning' (2020),
      www.louispoulsen.com/en/professional/about-us/louis-
      poulsen-learning.
9   Jørstian and Munk Nielsen, *Light Years Ahead*, p. 215.
10   Ibid., 2019.
11   Verner Panton website, 'Exhibition Stand: Fritz Hansen & Louis
      Poulsen' (2021), www.verner-panton.com/en/collection
      /exhibition-stand-fritz-hansen-louis-poulsen.
12   'Louis Poulsen, Euroluce 2017: GamFratesi', *Frame*
      (5 October 2017), www.frameweb.com/project/louis-
      poulsen-euroluce-2017.
13   Jørstian and Munk Nielsen, *Light Years Ahead*, pp. 216–17.
14   Michael Sheridan, *The Furniture of Poul Kjærholm: Catalogue
      Raisonné* (New York, 2007), p. 14.
15   Malene Lytken, *Danish Lights—1920 to Now* (Copenhagen,
      2019), pp. 42–3.
16   Dansk Møbelkunst, 'An extraordinary PH lamp'
      (31 January 2020), www.dmk.dk/the-fluorescent-pendant-ph/;
      Jørstian and Munk Nielsen, *Light Years Ahead*, pp. 295–7.
17   Ida Præstegaard, 'Styling Danish Life: Exhibition in Tokyo',
      LP Nyt, no. 580 (2005); 'Styling Danish Life Exhibition', IM
      Internet Museum, www.museum.or.jp/event/19404.
18   Jørstian and Munk Nielsen, *Light Years Ahead*, p. 237.
19   Ibid., p. 270.
20   Tin Jørstian and Poul Erik Nielsen, *PH 100 Lys og Design*
      (exhibition brochure).
21   Koldinghus, 'PH-Lampen 1924–2011' (3 November 2011).
      Accessed via Wayback Machine, www.web.archive.org/
      web/20111103111601/http://www.koldinghus.dk/Default.
      aspx?ID=3690; author's interview with Lisbeth Mansfeldt
      (28 June 2023).
22   'PHs lamper udstilles på Koldinghus', *Vejle Amts Folkeblad*
      (12 December 2021), www.vafo.dk/boerkop/phs-lamper-
      udstilles-paa-koldinghus.
23   Author's interview with Lisbeth Mansfeldt (5 July 2023).
24   Koldinghus, 'PH-Lampen 1924–2011'.
25   Tivoli press release, 'Poul Henningsen in Tivoli: Exhibition Marks
      125th Anniversary of Poul Henningsen's Birth' (22 January 2019),
      www.tivoli.dk/en/om/presse/pressemeddelelser/2019/ph-i-
      tivoli-udstilling.
26   Vitra Design Museum, 'Verner Panton: The Collected Works
      05.02.2000–12.06.2000' (2017), www.design-museum.de/en/
      exhibitions/detailpages/verner-panton.html.
27   Carin Panton von Halem and Stine Liv Buur, 'Verner Panton:
      Colouring a New World', Vitra (17 January 2022), www.vitra.com/
      en-gb/magazine/details/colouring-a-new-world.
28   Trapholt, 'Arne Jacobsen: Designing Denmark' (2020),
      www.trapholt.dk/en/arne-jacobsen/.
29   Tim Anscombe-Bell, 'Horns, tentacles and spikes: Louis
      Poulsen plays with its iconic lighting designs in new
      collaboration', *Wallpaper** (8 June 2023); author's interview with
      Breanna Box and Peter Dupont (3 July 2023).
30   Lisbeth Mansfeldt (28 June 2023).
31   Anne Hedegaard, 'Vejen vil lave museum for lysmageren P.H.',
      JydskeVestkysten (2 February 2010), www.jv.dk/vejen/vejen-vil-
      lave-museum-for-lysmageren-p-h.
32   Henning Larsen Architects, 'PH Museum' (22 April 2012). Ac-
      cessed via Wayback Machine, www.web.archive.org/web/
      20120422213140/https://henninglarsen.com/projects/1100-
      1199/1150-ph-museum.aspx.

BIBLIOGRAPHY

ARTICLES

Note: LP Nyt *is a monthly magazine published by Louis Poulsen (1941–2012).*

3daysofdesign, '*Bo Bedre*'s Design Awards 2022' [news post] (2022), www.3daysofdesign.dk/post/bo-bedres-design-awards-2022.

&Tradition, 'Langelinie Pavilion, Restaurant & Events' (2020), www.andtradition.com/journal/langelinie-pavilion.

Anscombe-Bell, Tim, 'Horns, tentacles and spikes: Louis Poulsen plays with its iconic lighting designs in new collaboration', *Wallpaper** (8 June 2023).

Arne Jacobsen Design, 'AJ Lamp' (2022), www.arnejacobsen.com/works/aj-lamp.

–––, 'House of the Future' (2022), www.arnejacobsen.com/works/house-of-the-future/.

–––, 'SAS Royal Hotel' (2022), www.arnejacobsen.com/works/sas-royal-hotel.

Asakura, Noriyuki, 'Japanese Light', *LP Nyt*, no. 559 (1998).

Bay, Carl Erik, 'Poul Henningsen', *Dansk Biografisk Leksikon* (accessed 24 July 2023), www.biografiskleksikon.lex.dk/Poul_Henningsen.

Beardsley, Eleanor, 'Tivoli Gardens Beckons on Denmark's Summer Nights', NPR (15 August 2012), www.npr.org/2012/08/15/158870832/on-denmarks-summer-nights-tivoli-gardens-beckon.

Beautyman, Mairi, 'Louis Poulsen Celebrates 60 Years with a Limited-Edition PH Artichoke Lamp', *Architectural Digest* (1 June 2018), www.architecturaldigest.com/story/louis-poulsen-poul-henningsen-artichoke-lamp-60-years.

Benson, Paula, 'Lights and lamps inspiration from film and TV', Film and Furniture' (6 July 2022), www.filmandfurniture.com/2022/07/lights-and-lamps-inspiration-from-film-and-tv/.

Bertoli, Rosa, 'Arne Jacobsen's lamps for St Catherine's College are now available from Louis Poulsen', *Wallpaper** (25 February 2023), www.wallpaper.com/design-interiors/arne-jacobsen-saint-catherine-college-cambridge-lamps-louis-poulsen.

Bonde, Lisbeth, 'Serial Lighting: 60 years of Nyt', *LP Nyt*, no. 570 (2001).

Boysen, Anne, 'Moonsetter', www.anneboysen.dk/#/moonsetter-louis-poulsen/.

Buhl Andersen, Pia, 'Nazigruppe ville dræbe dansk stjernearkitekt', *Politiken* (13 October 2012), www.politiken.dk/kultur/art5411366/Nazigruppe-ville-dr%C3%A6be-dansk-stjernearkitekt.

Carpenter, Wava, 'The Perennial Artichoke: Peeling back the layers of Poul Henningsen's timeless design', Pamono (2 February 2016), www.pamono.com/stories/poul-henningsen-artichoke-lamp-story.

Chan, TF, 'Own a piece of classic Danish furniture as seen in the Louisiana Museum of Modern Art', *Wallpaper** (22 August 2018), www.wallpaper.com/design/louisiana-museum-of-modern-art-60th-anniversary-reissues.

Chapman, Chris, 'Hall of Fame', *Wallpaper** (January/February 1998).

Cho, Jaehee, et al., 'White light-emitting diodes: History, progress, and future', *Laser & Photonics Reviews* (2 March 2017), www.onlinelibrary.wiley.com/doi/10.1002/lpor.201600147.

Christensen, Sverre Riis, 'A Real Advertising Tale', *LP Nyt*, no. 561 (1999).

Creative Denmark, 'Louis Poulsen: A Retake on the iconic PH 5' (25 October 2022), www.creativedenmark.com/cases/louis-poulsen-a-retake-on-the-iconic-ph-5.

Dahl, Holger, 'Arkens nye udendørs trækplaster er »ganske enkelt fremragende«', *Berlingske* (27 June 2021), www.berlingske.dk/design-mode-og-arkitektur/arkens-nye-udendoers-traekplaster-er-ganske-enkelt.

Danish Architecture Center, 'Stellings Hus: Undiscovered Icon on the Oldest Square in Copenhagen' (18 June 2021), www.dac.dk/en/knowledgebase/architecture/stellings-hus-stelling-house-undiscovered-icon-on-the-oldest-square-in-copenhagen/.

Dansk Møbeldesign, 'Louis Poulsen Lighting' (2012), www.danskmoebeldesign.dk/louis-poulsen-lighting.html.

–––, 'Udstilling om PH lamper på Koldinghus' (2012), www.danskmoebeldesign.dk/udstilling-om-ph-lamper-paa-koldinghus.html.

Dansk Møbelkunst, 'An extraordinary PH lamp' (31 January 2020), www.dmk.dk/the-fluorescent-pendant-ph/.

Danske Litteraturpriser ved Niels Jensen, 'PH Prisen' [year unknown], www.litteraturpriser.dk/divkult.htm#PH.

Daugaard, Stine, 'Spot på PH's lamper i Kolding', *Ingeniøren* (30 March 2012), ing.dk/artikel/spot-paa-phs-lamper-i-kolding.

De Waal, Alan, 'Lighting Culture', *LP Nyt*, no. 561 (1999).

–––, 'Panton's Universe', *LP Nyt*, no. 562 (1999).

Demetriou, Danielle, '5x5: Nendo', *Wallpaper** (October 2021).

Ekman, Ulf, 'Louis Poulsen & Co 100 år', *LP Nyt*, no. 380 (1973).

Fison, Lizzie, 'Clara von Zweigbergk's colourful lamps recall hot air balloons and carousels' (2 June 2017), www.dezeen.com/2017/06/02/clara-von-zweigbergk-louis-poulsen-colourful-lamps-hot-air-balloons-carousels/.

Flood, Alison, 'Terry Pratchett estate backs Jack Monroe's idea for "Vimes Boots" poverty index', *Guardian* (26 January 2022), www.theguardian.com/books/2022/jan/26/terry-pratchett-jack-monroe-vimes-boots-poverty-index.

Fritz Hansen, 'St Catherine's College' (2019), www.fritzhansen.com/en/Inspiration/Projects/St-Catherines-College-Oxford.

Garnett, Natasha, 'Italian Modern: The Gallerist Nina Yashar', *New York Times* (29 October 2014), www.nytimes.com/2014/10/29/t-magazine/italian-modern.html.

Griffiths, Alyn, 'Cosmic rays: Artist Olafur Eliasson scales down, shapes up and finds an inner light', *Wallpaper** (May 2019).

Hamilton, Ben, 'Remembering Tivoli's founder: a showman with a fondness for champagne and jazzy waistcoats', *CPH Post* (23 May 2017), www.cphpost.dk/2017-05-23/history/tivoli.

Hammond, George, 'Design classic: PH Artichoke lamp', *Financial Times* (23 March 2018), www.ft.com/content/793f91d4-2798-11e8-9274-2b13fccdc744.

Hedegaard, Anne, 'Vejen vil lave museum for lysmageren P.H.', *JydskeVestkysten* (2 February 2010), www.jv.dk/vejen/vejen-vil-lave-museum-for-lysmageren-p-h.

Hedegaard, Lars, 'The First 125 Years', *LP Nyt*, no. 561 (1999).

Henning Larsen Architects, 'PH Museum' (22 April 2012). Accessed via Wayback Machine, www.web.archive.org/web/2012 0422213140/https://henninglarsen.com/projects/1100-1199/1150-ph-museum.aspx.

Heward, John, 'Langeliniepavillonen / The Langelinie Pavilion', *Danish Design Review* (4 December 2018), www.danishdesignreview. com/kbhnotes/2018/12/12/langelinie pavillonen-the-langelinie-pavilion.

Hirst, Arlene, 'As Traditional Bulbs Fade Out, LED Lights Keep Improving', *New York Times* (3 May 2023), www.nytimes.com/2023/05/03/style/led-lights-improving.html.

House of Finn Juhl, 'Timeline' [the story of Finn Juhl] (2022), www.finnjuhl.com/about/timeline.

In-Light Scandinavia, 'Mogens Koch' (2020), www.in-light.dk/designre/mogens-koch.

Iversen, Kasper, 'PH-lampen: Fra politisk statement til sikkert valg', *Politiken* (3 April 2015), www.politiken.dk/kultur/design/art5572179/PH-lampen-Fra-politisk-statement-til-sikkert-valg.

Jelsbak, Torben, 'From Bauhaus to Our House—*Kritisk Revy*, Popular Culture, and the Roots of "Scandinavian Design"', in Benedikt Hjartarson, et al., eds, *A Cultural History of the Avant-Garde in the Nordic Countries 1925–1950* (Leiden, 2019).

Krause, Reinhard, 'Leuchtendes Beispiel: Vilhelm Lauritzen und seine ikonischen Möbel', *Architectural Digest Deutschland* (1 December 2011), www.ad-magazin.de/article/ikone-vilhelm-lauritzen.

Lauritzen, Vilhelm, and Poul Henningsen, 'Idealisme og honorar', *LP Nyt*, no. 110 (1951).

Lazure-Guinard, Catherine, 'LC Shutters by Louise Campbell', Nordic Design (27 February 2012), www.nordicdesign.ca/lc-shutters-by-louise-campbell/.

Logger, Koos, and Ingrid Stadler, 'The fascinating life of the PH Tennis Lamps at the K.B. Hallen in Copenhagen', Palainco (18 March 2019), www.palainco.com/discover/item/k-b-hallen-copenhagen-ph-tennis-lamps.

Louis Poulsen, 'A Lamp is Born', *Reflections*, no. 2 (2017).

–––, advertisement for Verner Panton's Panthella lamp, *LP Nyt*, no. 355 (1971).

–––, 'Alfred Homann' (2019), www.louis poulsen.com/en-gb/private/about-us/designers/alfred-homann.

–––, 'Arne Jacobsen' (2018), www.louis poulsen.com/en-gb/private/about-us/designers/arne-jacobsen.

–––, 'Campbell Pendant', *LP Nyt*, no. 579 (2004).

–––, 'New Fixtures in Light and Unpretentious Design', *LP Nyt*, no. 585 (2007).

–––, 'Øivind Slaatto's Patera Silver', *Reflections*, no. 5 (2019).

–––, 'The PH Artichoke's new little brother', *LP Nyt*, no. 572 (2002).

–––, 'PH in Tivoli', *Reflections*, no. 6 (2019), www.catalogue.louispoulsen.com/UK/louis-poulsen-reflections-6/.

–––, 'PH Reflections', *Reflections*, no. 3 (2018), www.catalogue.louispoulsen.com/UK/louis-poulsen-reflections-3.

–––, 'PH Septima: Finding a Lost Icon', *Reflections*, no. 8 (2020).

–––, 'Spotlight on Christian Flindt', *Reflections*, no. 4 (2018).

–––, 'Vilhelm Lauritzen' (2018), www.louis-poulsen.com/en-gb/private/about-us/designers/vilhelm-lauritzen.

Madsen, Fred, 'Louis Poulsen tænder nyt lys i Vejen', *Berlingske* (13 April 2005), www.berlingske.dk/business/louis-poulsen-taender-nyt-lys-i-vejen.

Martin, Hannah, 'The Story Behind the Revolutionary Artichoke Light', *Architectural Digest* (30 June 2018), www.architectural digest.com/story/the-story-behind-the-revolutionary-artichoke-light.

Mende, Andrea, 'Design that supports people' [Lise Vester interview] Stylepark (18 April 2023), www.stylepark.com/en/news/lise-vester-design-light-interview-euroluce-3daysofdesign-stylepark-magazin.

Møller, Svend Erik, Preben Willmann and Thomas Winding, eds, 'Til en afveksling har PH', *LP Nyt*, no. 273 (1964).

Munch, Anders V., 'Conspicuously Quotidian: Poul Henningsen on Bauhaus and the Art of Promoting Danish Modern', *Tahiti* (2021), www.tahiti.journal.fi/article/view/111940/65714.

Nelsen, Arthur, 'Europe to ban halogen lightbulbs', *Guardian* (23 August 2018), www.theguardian.com/environment/2018/aug/23/europe-to-ban-halogen-lightbulbs.

nendo, 'NJP table' (2015), www.nendo.jp/en/works/njp-table-2/.

O'Kelly, Emma, 'Great Dane', *Wallpaper** (April 2001).

Panton von Halem, Carin, and Stine Liv Buur, 'Verner Panton: Colouring a New World', Vitra (17 January 2022), www.vitra.com/en-gb/magazine/details/colouring-a-new-world.

Pedersen, Jørgen, 'The PH lamp and its numbers', *LP Nyt*, no. 566 (2000).

–––, 'Poul Henningsen's logarithmic spiral', *LP Nyt*, no. 567 (2000).

'PHs lamper udstilles på Koldinghus', *Vejle Amts Folkeblad* (12 December 2021), www.vafo.dk/boerkop/phs-lamper-udstilles-paa-koldinghus.

Præstegaard, Ida, 'Enigma', *LP Nyt*, no. 576 (2003).

–––, 'The first PH Artichokes are still there', *LP Nyt*, no. 572 (2002).

–––, 'From unconventional idea to reality', *LP Nyt*, no. 581 (2005).

–––, 'Light must be honest: Interview with Mads Odgård', *LP Lyt*, no. 574 (2003).

293

---, 'The PH lamps in Tivoli Gardens are rotating again', *LP Nyt*, no. 586 (2008).

---, 'Styling Danish Life: Exhibition in Tokyo', *LP Nyt*, no. 580 (2005).

Ramirez, Ainissa, 'Tungsten's Brilliant, Hidden History', *American Scientist* (27 January 2020), www.americanscientist.org/article/tungstens-brilliant-hidden-history.

Ronan, Alex, 'The Lighting Fixture that Inspired a High-Stakes Heist: The PH Artichoke', *Dwell* (15 February 2015), www.dwell.com/article/the-lighting-fixture-that-inspired-a-high-stakes-heist-the-ph-artichoke-7aa5d797.

Roux, Caroline, 'Prism Break: Louise Campbell's "Nervous" chandelier for Baccarat pushed both designer and manufacturer to the limit', *Wallpaper** (May 2013).

SAGA Space Architects, 'LUNARK—Building and Testing a Moon Home for Everyone' [press release] (2020), www.docs.google.com/document/d/16eq25FRIyGIqHEtbNsfrYTeUn2wQF4imJeLtULtlwj0.

Savoy Helsinki, 'Savoy Restaurant' (2020), www.savoyhelsinki.fi/restaurant.

Schjeldahl, Peter, 'Uncluttered: An Olafur Eliasson retrospective', *New Yorker* (21 April 2008), www.newyorker.com/magazine/2008/04/28/uncluttered.

Science History Institute, 'Critical Metals: The Chemistry of Light', Google Arts & Culture (2022), www.artsandculture.google.com/story/critical-metals-the-chemistry-of-light-science-history-institute/9AWhIBWIbZ1jUQ.

Strauss, Cindi, 'Poul Henningsen', in Sarah Schleuning and Cindi Strauss, eds, *Electrifying Design: A Century of Lighting* (Houston, 2021).

Tabuchi, Hiroko, 'It's Official: Stores Can No Longer Sell Most Incandescent Lights', *New York Times* (1 August 2023), www.nytimes.com/2023/08/01/climate/incandescent-light-bulb-ban-leds.html.

Thomson, C. Claire, 'Lamps, Light, and Enlightenment: Poul Henningsen's Denmark and Ole Roos' PH Light', *Kosmorama* (31 May 2013), www.kosmorama.org/en/kosmorama/artikler/lamps-light-and-enlightenment-poul-henningsens-denmark-and-ole-roos-ph-light.

Tivoli, 'Poul Henningsen in Tivoli: Exhibition Marks 125th Anniversary of Poul Henningsen's Birth' [press release] (22 January 2019), www.tivoli.dk/en/om/presse/pressemeddelelser/2019/ph-i-tivoli-udstilling.

'Verner Panton', *Domus* (2021), www.domusweb.it/en/biographies/verner-panton.html.

Vilhelm Lauritzen Architects, 'The Radio House' (2022), www.vilhelmlauritzen.com/project/radiohouse.

Voltelen, Mogens, 'PH lampen i histories belysning', *LP Nyt*, no. 112 (1951).

Waddoups, Ryan, 'Designer of the Day: Anne Boysen', *Surface* (19 December 2022), www.surfacemag.com/articles/anne-boysen-designer-day/.

BOOKS AND CATALOGUES

Bailey, Diane, *How the Light Bulb Changed History* (North Mankato, Minn., 2015).

Bundegaard, Christian, *100 Years of Danish Modern: Vilhelm Lauritzen Architects* (Copenhagen, 2022).

Burrows, Edwin G. *The Finest Building in America: The New York Crystal Palace 1853–1858* (New York, 2018).

Dybdahl, Lars, ed., *101 Danish Design Icons* (Berlin, 2016).

Engholm, Ida, and Anders Michelsen, *Verner Panton* (London, 2018).

Friedel, Robert, and Paul B. Israel, Edison's *Electric Light: The Art of Invention* (Baltimore, 2010).

Gelfer-Jørgensen, Mirjam, *Influences from Japan in Danish Art and Design 1870–2010* (Copenhagen, 2013).

Hertel, Hans, *Good Light* (Copenhagen, 2016).

Isenstadt, Sandy, *Electric Light: An Architectural History* (Cambridge, Mass., 2018).

Jørstian, Tina, and Poul Erik Munk Nielsen, eds, *Light Years Ahead: The Story of the PH Lamp* (Copenhagen, 1994).

Keiding Martin, and Kim Dirckinck-Holmfeld, *Utzon and the New Tradition* (Copenhagen, 2005).

Kingsley, Patrick, *How to Be Danish: A Journey to the Cultural Heart of Denmark* (London, 2012).

Levin, Anna, *Incandescent: We Need to Talk about Light* (Salford, UK, 2019).

Louis Poulsen, Louis Poulsen *Sustainability Report 2021* (Copenhagen, 2022).

---, Louis Poulsen *Sustainability Report 2022* (Copenhagen, 2023).

Lytken, Malene, *Danish Lights—1920 to Now* (Copenhagen, 2019).

McCarter, Robert, *Aalto* (London, 2014).

Moss, Murray, *Georg Jensen: Reflections* (New York, 2014).

Mussari, Mark, *Danish Modern: Between Art and Design* (London, 2016).

PH 100 Lys og Design (Copenhagen, 1994).

Sheridan, Michael, *Louisiana: Architecture and Landscape* (Humlebæk, 2017).

–––, *The Furniture of Poul Kjærholm: Catalogue Raisonné* (New York, 2007).

Te Duits, Thimo, ed., *The Origin of Things: Sketches, Models, Prototypes* (Rotterdam, 2003).

Thau, Carsten, and Kjeld Vindum, *Arne Jacobsen* (Copenhagen, 1998).

EXHIBITIONS

Koldinghus, 'PH-Lampen 1924–2011' (3 November 2011). Accessed via Wayback Machine, www.web.archive.org/web/2011 1103111601/http://www.koldinghus.dk/Default.aspx?ID=3690.

London Design Biennale, 'Denmark & Switzerland: Blue Nomad' (2023), www.londondesignbiennale.com/pavilions/2023/denmark-switzerland.

'Louis Poulsen, Euroluce 2017: GamFratesi', *Frame* (5 October 2017), www.frameweb.com/project/louis-poulsen-euroluce-2017.

'Styling Danish Life Exhibition' [2004 exhib. in Tokyo], IM Internet Museum, www.museum.or.jp/event/19404.

Trapholt, 'Arne Jacobsen: Designing Denmark' (2020), www.trapholt.dk/en/arne-jacobsen/.

Utzon Center, 'A Space Saga: Mar 31st 2023 to Sep 3rd 2023' (2023), www.utzoncenter.dk/en/exhibition/a-space-saga-10346.

Verner Panton—Official, 'Exhibition Stand: Fritz Hansen & Louis Poulsen' [1972 exhibition] (2021), www.verner-panton.com/en/collection/exhibition-stand-fritz-hansen-louis-poulsen.

Vitra Design Museum, 'Verner Panton: The Collected Works 05.02.2000—12.06.2000' (2017), www.design-museum.de/en/exhibitions/detailpages/verner-panton.html.

INTERVIEWS WITH THE AUTHOR

Breanna Box and Peter Dupont, co-founders of Heven (3 July 2023).

Anne Boysen, architect and designer (5 July 2023).

Louise Campbell, designer (12 July 2023).

Ellen Dahl, former communications consultant at Tivoli (28 June 2023).

Monique Faber, director of product and design at Louis Poulsen (28 and 29 June 2023).

Christian Flindt, designer (11 July 2023).

Charlotte June Henningsen, Peter Johansen and Louise Danneskiold-Samsøe, Poul Henningsen's heirs (28 June 2023).

Lisbeth Mansfeldt, retired brand manager at Louis Poulsen (28 June and 5 July 2023).

Søren Mygind Eskildsen, CEO at Louis Poulsen (29 June 2023).

Mads Odgård, designer (3 July 2023).

Ulla Riemer, head of international training and education at Louis Poulsen (12 July 2023).

Øivind Slaatto, designer (5 July 2023).

Kristine Stilling Pedersen, supply chain planner at Louis Poulsen (27 June 2023).

Yoichi Nishio, editor-in-chief of *Casa BRUTUS* (19 September 2023).

LAMP AUCTION AND SALE LOT ENTRIES

Bonhams, 'Lot 46W. Poul Henningsen (1894–1967): Important Pre-Production Artichoke Ceiling Light from the Langelinie Pavilion' (2018), www.bonhams.com/auction/24848/lot/46/poul-henningsen-1894-1967-important-pre-production-artichoke-ceiling-light-from-the-langelinie-pavilion1958for-louis-poulsen-solid-copper-nickel-plated-brass-pale-pink-reflective-interior-paint-plastic-top-plate-engraved-lpheight-26in-66cm-diameter-31in-79cm/.

Christie's, 'Poul Henningsen (1894–1967). A rare "Spiral" ceiling light: Lot Essay' (3 October 2017), www.christies.com/en/lot/lot-6101630.

Dansk Møbelkunst, 'Hans J. Wegner table lamp for Aarhus City Hall' (2022), www.dmk.dk/item/hans-wegner-table-lamp-aarhus-city-hall/.

–––, 'Vilhelm Lauritzen: "Universal" Pendant' (2021), www.dmk.dk/item/vilhelm-lauritzen-the-universal-pendant-1929-louis-poulsen/.

Pamono, 'Vintage Model Opala Pendant Lamp by Hans J. Wegner for Louis Poulsen' [year unknown], www.pamono.co.uk/vintage-model-opala-pendant-lamp-by-hans-j-wegner-for-louis-poulsen.

Phillips, '114. Poul Henningsen: "The House of the Future" ceiling light' (17 November 2011), www.phillips.com/detail/poul-henningsen/UK050311/114.

–––, '115. Poul Henningsen: Exceptional and large "Spiral" wall light, for the Scala cinema and concert hall, Århus Theater, Århus, Denmark' (17 November 2011), www.phillips.com/detail/poul-henningsen/UK050311/115.

Visavu, 'Vilhelm Lauritzen pair of Guldpendel lamps, Denmark 1955' (2020), www.visavu.nl/portfolio/vilhelm-lauritzen-pair-of-guldpendel-lamps-denmark-1955/.

For lamps mentioned in this book that are still in production, see:

www.louispoulsen.com.

www.artek.fi (Pendant A330S 'Golden Bell').

www.northseadesign.nl (MK 114 Mogens Koch In-light Pendant Lamp).

VIDEOES AND SOCIAL MEDIA POSTS

Adam Christopher Design, 'Design Classic 1960 Verner Panton the Moon Pendant Review', YouTube (uploaded 23 August 2017), www.youtube.com/watch?v=vAYRAmGtXuM.

Be Original Americas and Louis Poulsen, 'Be Original Americas × Louis Poulsen: Conversation with Øivind Slaatto', YouTube (uploaded 29 July 2020), www.youtube.com/watch?v=-4KWgkN5qUo.

Louis Poulsen, 'LC Shutters—Pendant by Louise Campbell', YouTube (uploaded 1 March 2012), www.youtube.com/watch?v=4bUg5T8hVcE.

–––, 'Louis Poulsen Learning' (2020) www.louispoulsen.com/en/professional/about-us/louis-poulsen-learning.

–––, 'LP Cité', Vimeo (uploaded 19 April 2016), www.vimeo.com/163410137.

–––, 'NJP—Designed by nendo', YouTube (uploaded 3 January 2018), www.youtube.com/watch?v=h5iDIJo82Mg.

–––, 'PH: Philosophy of light', YouTube (3 videos of original documentary *PH lys*, 1964; uploaded 16 September 2008), www.youtube.com/watch?v=CFB4qgGTtMo, www.youtube.com/watch?v=t7nHqYzjYfw, www.youtube.com/watch?v=8ZpKg24_UKI.

–––, 'Thoughts about Cirque—Designed by Clara von Zweigbergk—Produced by Louis Poulsen', YouTube (uploaded 23 March 2018), www.youtube.com/watch?v=Rvwfe4uqF8w.
Oda Collection, 'Life at Oda's Residence, Vol. 6—Noritsugu Oda's Special Interview', YouTube (uploaded 1 February 2022), www.youtube.com/watch?v=CVcUXsSWgP0.

Okholm Lighting, 'Wegnerlygten' (2019), www.okholm-lighting.dk/produkter-visning/udendorsbelysning/wegnerlygten.

Rawsthorn, Alice, 'Design and light' [Instagram post] (22 November 2016), www.instagram.com/p/BNGsBL9AZeA/?taken-by=alice.rawsthorn.

–––, 'Poul Henningsen' [series of Instagram posts] (4–10 September 2020), www.instagram.com/p/BYm8AfzAeYt/?taken-by=alice.rawsthorn.

SAGA Space Architects, 'LUNARK × Louis Poulsen', Vimeo (uploaded 5 May 2021), www.vimeo.com/545503755.

Vester, Lise, 'Lise Vester Studio 2022', YouTube (uploaded 10 May 2022), www.youtube.com/watch?v=r9VskD6GBbY.

–––, 'The Making of *Fabrikkens Idea Generator*' [Instagram post] (11 October 2022), www.instagram.com/p/CjkWBmXjUSM.

WEBSITES

Arne Jacobsen Design, www.arnejacobsen.com.

–––, 'Authorized Partners' (2022), www.arnejacobsen.com/authenticity/authorized-partners.

Lise Vester, www.lisevester.dk.

Little Sun, www.littlesun.org/about/mission/.

Louis Poulsen, www.louispoulsen.com.

Studio Olafur Eliasson, 'Ice Watch, 2014' (2023), www.olafureliasson.net/artwork/ice-watch-2014/.

–––, 'The Weather Project, 2003' (2023), www.olafureliasson.net/artwork/the-weather-project-2003/.

Studio Other Spaces, www.studioother spaces.net.

Tivoli, www.tivoli.dk/en/om/tivolis-historie.

Uchiyama Design, www.uchiyama-design.jp/works.

INDEX

PICTURE CREDITS

Unless otherwise noted below, all images are courtesy and copyright © Louis Poulsen.
T – Top, B – Bottom, C – Centre, L – Left, R – Right.

Pages 27, 32, 49, 51, 67 and 108 © Photo: Bent Ryberg; pages 28, 29 and 122 © Photo: Royal Danish Library – Danish National Art Library; pages 34 and 35 © Photo: David Zidlicky; page 62 © Design Musuem Danmark; page 63 © Alvar Aalto Foundation; pages 68, 70 TL, 70 TR, 70 BL, 70 BR and 89 © SFC / Det Danske Filminstitut; pages 82 L, 82 R and 268 © Tivoli; page 87 © Photo: Emil Christensen; page 90 Photographer: Paul Koslowski; pages 94 and 97 © SAGA Space Architects; page 98 © Lise Vester Studio // Kristian Holm; pages 102 and 104 B © Langelinie Pavillonen; page 116 Photo: Kjeld Helmer Petersen; pages 120 and 123 © Photo: Dissing+Weitling; pages 124, 125, 126, 127, 128 T and 128 B Photo: Aage Strüwing © Jørgen Strüwing; page 138 © Colin Westwood / RIBA Collections; page 139 © Fritz Hansen / Egon Gade; pages 141 and 151 © Rasmus Hjortshøj – Vilhelm Lauritzen Arkitekter; pages 142 T and 142 B © Vilhelm Lauritzen Arkitekter – Royal Danish Library – Danish National Art Library; page 143 © Rune Buch; page 144 © Vilhelm Lauritzen Arkitekter – Royal Danish Library; pages 145 and 152 © Vilhelm Lauritzen Arkitekter; pages 154, 156 T and 156 B © Louisiana Museum of Modern Art // Fotograf: Jesper Høm; pages 162, 164, 165, 167, 171, 173 T, 173 B, 264 and 265 © Verner Panton Design AG; pages 188 and 189 Photo: Udo Kowalski; pages 200 L and 200 R © Photographer: Piotr Topperzer; page 241 T Photo: Silke Heneka / Studio Olafur Eliasson The A.P. Møller and Chastine Mc-Kinney Møller Foundation © 2004 Olafur Eliasson; page 241 B Photo: Lars Schmidt The A.P. Møller and Chastine Mc-Kinney Møller Foundation © 2004 Olafur Eliasson; page 242 © Harpa; page 243 Photo: Jens Ziehe, Courtesy of the artist; neugerriemschneider, Berlin; Tanya Bonakdar Gallery, New York / Los Angeles © 2003 Olafur Eliasson; page 270 © Photo: Ole Helweg; pages 276 and 277 © Kenneth Stjernegaard; pages 280 © Henning Larsen Architects

Every reasonable effort has been made to acknowledge the ownership of copyright for photographs included in this volume. Any errors are inadvertent and will be corrected in subsequent editions provided notification is sent in writing to the publisher.

ACKNOWLEDGEMENTS

A heartfelt thank you to the Louis Poulsen team, who welcomed me with open arms and readily offered their wisdom and expertise, especially to Sarah Lærke Stevens, who took a leap of faith in putting me forward for this assignment, and Thea Raben, for her expert coordination. Further thanks are due to the many Louis Poulsen collaborators who contributed their voices.

I am immensely grateful to Emilia Terragni, Phaidon's associate publisher, and Sophie Hodgkin, senior editor. Without their trust, determination, and infinite patience, this first-time book author would have been entirely lost.

I am fortunate to have many allies among Denmark's creative community, who have inspired my affection for the country's design history and made Copenhagen feel like a second home: in particular, my gratitude goes to Frederik Bille Brahe, Jesper Elg, Nanna Hjortenberg, Julius Værnes Iversen, Mathias Mentze and Alexander V Ottenstein, Dorthe Steffensen, and David Thulstrup and Martin Jacob Nielsen.

For their enthusiastic support and invaluable friendship, I would also like to thank Rosa Bertoli, Richard and Marian Bott, Andrew Bristow and Nathan Pell, Sujata Burman, Tony Chambers, Maria Cristina Didero, Ingar Dragset, Michael Elmgreen, Adam Nathaniel Furman, Nolan Giles and Hyo Jung Lee, David Graver, Holly Hay, Jakob Kudsk Steensen and Liz Kircher, Harriet Lloyd-Smith, Lauren Ho, Pei-Ru Keh, Jessica Klingelfuss, Christina and John Murphy, Josef O'Connor, Amy Serafin, and Tom Phillips.

My final thanks go to my family, most of all my father Wai-Leung Chan and my mother Iannie Kou, for their constant encouragement and enduring love.

Phaidon Press Limited
2 Cooperage Yard
London E15 2QR

Phaidon Press Inc.
111 Broadway
New York, NY 10006

phaidon.com

First published 2024
© 2024 Phaidon Press Limited

ISBN 978 1 83866 780 1 (Trade Edition)
ISBN 978 1 83866 864 8 (Louis Poulsen
Edition)

A CIP catalogue record for this book is
available from the British Library and the
Library of Congress.

All rights reserved. No part of this
publication may be reproduced, stored
in a retrieval system or transmitted, in
any form or by any means, electronic,
mechanical, photocopying, recording or
otherwise, without the written permission
of Phaidon Press Limited.

Commissioning Editor: Emilia Terragni
Project Editor: Sophie Hodgkin
Production Controller: Lily Rodgers
Design: Studio Claus Due

The Publisher would like to thank Jane
Birch, Emma Caddy, Sarah Lærke Stevens,
Joanne Murray, Thea Raben and Dana
Tanaka-Lingg for their contributions to
the book.

Printed in China